Dian Fossey

ANIMAL RIGHTS ACTIVIST AND PROTECTOR OF MOUNTAIN GORILLAS

By Diane Dakers

Crabtree Publishing Company
www.crabtreebooks.com

🌳 Crabtree Publishing Company
www.crabtreebooks.com

Author: Diane Dakers
Publishing plan research and development:
    Reagan Miller
Project coordinator: Mark Sachner,
Editors: Mark Sachner, Lynn Peppas
Indexer: Gini Holland
Editorial director: Kathy Middleton
Photo research: Ruth Owen
Designer: Westgraphix/Tammy West
Production: Kim Richardson
Prepress technician: Ken Wright
Print coordinator: Kathy Berti

Produced by Water Buffalo Books

Publisher's note:
All quotations in this book come from original sources and contain the spelling and grammatical inconsistencies of the original text. Some of the quotations may also contain terms that are no longer in use and may be considered inappropriate or offensive. The use of such terms is for the sake of preserving the historical and literary accuracy of the sources and should not be seen as encouraging or endorsing the use of such terms today.

Photographs and reproductions
Alamy: © Liam White: pp. 1, 4 (top), 13, 15, 56, 75 (bottom), 83, 86–87; © Everett Collection Historical: p. 25; © ZUMA Press Inc.: p. 29 (bottom); © Susanna Bennett: p. 40; © Ariadne Van Zandbergen: pp. 48–49; © Robert Harding: p. 55; © Marcin Jamkowski/Adventure Pictures: p. 79; © A & J Visage: p. 84 (top); **Bridgeman Images:** Veit, Peter G. / National Geographic Creative / Bridgeman Images: cover (background); **Corbis:** © Yann Arthus-Bertrand: cover (foreground), pp. 5, 43, 69, 76; © Bettmann: p. 38; **Cosmographics:** © p. 51; **FLPA:** © Suzi Eszterhas/Minden Pictures: pp. 28, 45; © Jean-Eric Fabre/Biosphoto: pp. 59, 60; © Ariadne Van Zandbergen: p. 77; © Konrad Wothe: p. 99; **Getty Images:** © Terence Spencer: p. 36; © Neil Selkirk: p. 89 (bottom); **Press Association Images:** © Brenton Kelly: p. 93 (top); **Public Domain:** pp. 9 (bottom), 16–17, 97 (bottom); **Rex:** © SIPA PRESS: pp. 42, 64; © Universal/courtesy Everett Collection: p. 91; **Shutterstock:** pp. 4 (bottom), 7, 10, 11, 24, 29 (top), 31, 33, 34, 53, 63, 72, 75 (top), 84 (bottom), 89 (top), 93 (bottom), 103; © Palenque: p. 97 (top); © LMSpencer: p. 97 (center); © atm2003: p. 98; © Snap2Art: p. 100; **Wikipedia/Creative Commons:** pp. 9 (top), 19, 22, 26, 30, 47, 95.

Library and Archives Canada Cataloguing in Publication

Dakers, Diane, author
    Dian Fossey : animal rights activist and protector of mountain / Diane Dakers.

(Crabtree groundbreaker biographies)
Includes index.
Issued in print and electronic formats.
ISBN 978-0-7787-2563-3 (bound).--ISBN 978-0-7787-2565-7 (paperback).--ISBN 978-1-4271-8093-3 (html)

    1. Fossey, Dian--Juvenile literature. 2. Primatologists--United States--Biography--Juvenile literature. 3. Animal rights activists--United States--Biography--Juvenile literature. I. Title. II. Series: Crabtree groundbreaker biographies

QL31.F68D35 2016   j599.884092   C2015-908720-1
                                        C2015-908721-X

Library of Congress Cataloging-in-Publication Data

Names: Dakers, Diane, author.
Title: Dian Fossey : animal rights activist and protector of mountain
    gorillas / Diane Dakers.
Description: New York, New York : Crabtree Publishing, [2016] |
    Series:
    Crabtree groundbreaker biographies | Includes index. | Description
    based on print version record and CIP data provided by publisher;
    resource not viewed.
Identifiers: LCCN 2015050157 (print) | LCCN 2015049885 (ebook) |
    ISBN
    9781427180933 (electronic HTML) | ISBN 9780778725633
    (reinforced library
    binding : alk. paper) | ISBN 9780778725657 (pbk. : alk. paper)
Subjects: LCSH: Fossey, Dian--Juvenile literature. | Women
    primatologists--United States--Biography--Juvenile literature. |
    Primatologists--United States--Biography--Juvenile literature. |
    Gorilla--Rwanda--Juvenile literature.
Classification: LCC QL31.F65 (print) | LCC QL31.F65 D35 2016
    (ebook) | DDC
    599.884092--dc23
LC record available at http://lccn.loc.gov/2015050157

Crabtree Publishing Company
www.crabtreebooks.com   1-800-387-7650

Printed in Canada/022016/IH20151223

Published in Canada
Crabtree Publishing
616 Welland Ave.
St. Catharines, Ontario
L2M 5V6

Published in the United States
Crabtree Publishing
PMB16A
350 Fifth Ave., Suite 3308
New York, NY 10118

Published in the United Kingdom
Crabtree Publishing
Maritime House
Basin Road North, Hove
BN41 1WR

Published in Australia
Crabtree Publishing
386 Mt. Alexander Rd.
Ascot Vale (Melbourne)
VIC 3032

Contents

Below: A mountain gorilla rests within Virunga National Park in Africa. The park was founded primarily as a protected area for the endangered mountain gorillas that make their home in the Virunga Mountains. The Virungas run along the borders of Rwanda, the Democratic Republic of the Congo, and Uganda.

Inset, right: Dian Fossey was devoted to the study, protection, and preservation of mountain gorillas and their habitats. She shared a warmth and trust with these gentle animals that was unrivaled by most of her "human" relationships. In this photo, the baby gorilla with which Dian is playing is a little difficult to spot against the dark tree, but Dian's delight is hard to miss!

Chapter 1
"Gorilla Girl"

On April 3, 1966, Dian Fossey patiently waited for a chance to speak to one of her idols. Louis Leakey was the world's most famous archaeologist and paleontologist. He spent most of his time in Africa, where Dian had met him three years earlier. On this day, he happened to be giving a speech in Louisville, Kentucky, where Dian now lived. She desperately wanted to speak to Louis again, so she joined the line of admirers after his lecture. But would he remember her?

Dian Fossey is shown in Rwanda with members of her anti-poaching patrol. As her fight against poachers who trapped and killed mountain gorillas became increasingly aggressive, her methods included not only cutting and seizing snares and traps, but chasing and shooting at poachers.

FIELD NOTES

A paleontologist is a scientist who studies fossils to understand the history of humans, animals, and plants. An archaeologist studies the past, from the prehistoric past through recent times, primarily through the excavation, or digging up, of sites and the examination of artifacts and other remains left behind.

Dian's Brave New World

When it was Dian's turn to talk to Louis, her patience was rewarded. The world-famous scientist greeted her warmly. "Miss Fossey, isn't it?" he said. She was thrilled that Louis knew her.

At the time, Dian worked at a hospital for children with physical and developmental disabilities. Her passion, though, was for mountain gorillas. Her desire to see them in person was the reason for her trip to Africa three years earlier.

In 1963, on her way to see some of the elusive creatures, Dian and her guide had taken a side trip to Olduvai Gorge, Louis's legendary archaeological dig site. After a brief (and, for Dian, memorable) meeting with the renowned scientist, she carried on to her true destination— the mountainside habitat of the rare mountain gorilla.

Amazingly, thanks to a local tracker, Dian managed to spot some of the mysterious creatures. More amazingly, she managed to get close enough to photograph them.

Upon her return from Africa, Dian wrote a few newspaper articles about her encounter with the great apes. Now, she nervously handed the newspaper clippings to Louis. He was so impressed with Dian's photographs, he invited her to a breakfast meeting the following morning to continue their gorilla discussion. Of course, she agreed!

Louis was famous for his work with fossils, but he was also famous for launching the career of chimpanzee expert Jane Goodall. At his morning meeting with Dian, Louis told her he

One Big Happy Family

Genetics is the study of physical characteristics and other biological traits that appear and develop in life forms over vast periods of time. Genetically speaking, humans, chimpanzees, gorillas, and orangutans are members of the same family. That family, or group of related species, is called *hominidae*, the "great apes."

Western gorillas

Mountain gorilla

This family includes humans, chimpanzees, bonobos, which are closely related to chimps, two species of orangutans, and gorillas.

There are two main species, or types, of gorillas, western and eastern. Mountain gorillas are a type of eastern gorilla. As their name suggests, they live on the slopes of mountains. They have longer, shaggier coats than their lowland cousins.

Genetically, chimpanzees (and their close genetic relations, bonobos) are humans' closest relatives. These species share 98.8 percent of the same genetic information, known as DNA. Chimps and gorillas share 98.2 percent of their DNA. This means that, with a difference of only 1.2 percent between chimpanzees and humans, chimps' DNA is more closely related to ours than it is to gorillas'.

Bonobo

Meanwhile, the genes of humans and gorillas differ by just 1.6 percent. We differ from orangutans by 3 percent.

Just so you know, all human beings share 99.9 per cent of the same genetic code. This means that genetically, every person is pretty much the same!

Chimpanzee

Orangutan mother and baby

was looking for another researcher. This time, he was seeking someone to undertake a long-term study of mountain gorillas. He asked Dian if she would like to be that person.

She was stunned by the offer—she had no formal training, and she was 34 years old. Surely she was too old and inexperienced for such a project.

Louis told Dian that her maturity was an advantage and that her passion was more important than scientific training. "I have no use

FAMOUS FOSSIL FAMILY

Louis Leakey was born in Kenya in 1903. His parents were British missionaries who worked with Kenya's largest tribal group, the Kikuyu. Louis spoke Kikuyu before he spoke English. When he was 13, he was initiated into the tribe and given the name Wakaruigi, or "Son of the sparrow hawk."

As a child, Louis often wandered through the wilderness. He occasionally found arrowheads and stone tools, which sparked his interest in the history of humanity.

When he was a 21-year-old anthropology student, Louis went on his first archaeological dig in Africa. At the time, experts believed humanity had originated in Asia. Louis believed it had begun in Africa.

In 1931, he began his work at Olduvai Gorge in Tanzania, an area rich in fossils. In 1936, he married Mary Nichols (also an anthropologist). Together, they made a number of important finds, including skulls, teeth, bones, and tools. These discoveries proved human ancestors had lived in Africa millions of years ago.

Louis also believed that long-term studies of great apes, which are genetically similar to humans, would teach scientists much about human evolution, which is the gradual development of humans over a long period of time. He commissioned Jane Goodall, Dian Fossey, and Birute Galdikas to undertake such studies.

Louis and Mary's son Richard and his wife Meave continue Louis's work today, as does granddaughter Louise. Louis Leakey died in 1972.

for over-trained people," he said. "I prefer people who are not specifically educated for this field, since they go into the work with open minds and without prejudice and preconceptions."

Dian jumped at the chance to spend time in the wilderness with mountain gorillas—it was a dream come true!

Eight months later, Dian Fossey arrived in Africa to start her study of the great apes, a passion that would consume 18 years of her life. Louis called her the "gorilla girl."

Anthropologists Mary and Louis Leakey with a tiny fossil specimen in 1962. Inset: a replica based on a fossilized skull discovered by Mary and unearthed by her and Louis in 1959. The skull was of an early ancestor of humans and dated back more than 1.7 million years.

The "Trimates"

Because of the close genetic relationships between humans, chimpanzees, gorillas, and orangutans, Louis Leakey believed that much could be learned about human evolution by studying the behavior of great apes in their natural habitats. To that end, in 1958, he commissioned Jane Goodall to study chimpanzees in Tanganyika (now Tanzania). In 1966, he hired Dian Fossey to observe mountain gorillas in the nations of Congo and Rwanda. And in 1971, he sponsored Birute Galdikas in a study of orangutans in Borneo. These three female researchers became known as "Leakey's Ladies," "Leakey's Angels," or—in a pun on "primate," which is a grouping of mammals that includes humans and apes—the "Trimates."

Gorilla Expert

During her years in Africa, Dian did more than observe gorillas. She also recognized that human activities threatened their survival as a species. She shared these facts of gorilla life with the world.

Over the years, Dian wrote four books and seven scientific papers about mountain gorilla behavior. She discovered they were curious, affectionate creatures that loved to socialize and play.

A mountain gorilla family in Africa. As Dian spent more time with mountain gorillas, she found them to be, in her words, "dignified, highly social, gentle giants, with individual personalities, and strong family relationships."

She learned much about what gorillas eat, how they spend their days, how they interact with each other, and what they "say" to each other. For more than a year, she recorded gorillas' vocalizations and discovered they make 16 or 17 clear and distinct sounds, each with its own meaning.

Dian, and the students who worked with her, also kept counts of the gorilla population in the Rwandan jungle. Through the 1970s and 1980s, these counts showed that gorilla numbers were drastically declining. That's because their habitat was being turned into farmland, and local people were killing them—often by accident, and sometimes on purpose. Dian predicted that, if nothing changed, mountain gorillas would be extinct before the end of the 20th century.

By this time, Dian was acknowledged as the world's leading mountain gorilla expert, so when she shared her prediction about the gorillas' bleak future, people listened. This led to one of the first coordinated conservation efforts in the world. Conservation is the act of preserving, protecting, and restoring the natural environment, including its habitats and wildlife. To help save the gentle beasts, some of Dian's colleagues launched education and tourism programs in the Rwandan jungle.

An aerial photograph of the border of Virunga National Park with fields on one side and woods on the other. This photo shows a striking contrast between the impact of cultivated farmland and the conservation of woodland that is home to mountain gorillas and other wildlife.

Dian, on the other hand, had her own techniques for protecting gorillas and dealing with the people who threatened them. Her sometimes-violent methods terrified the local African people. Eventually, her tactics became a cause of concern for everyone who knew her.

At the same time, many researchers questioned Dian's unusual study techniques. They felt her approach to her work was unscientific. Certainly nobody denied Dian's significant contributions to gorilla research, but as she spent more and more time alone in the jungle, even her supporters began to question her abilities—and her sanity.

BORN FREE

In 1956, in Kenya, an Austrian naturalist named Joy Adamson and her husband George took in an orphaned lion cub. They named the little one Elsa, raised her, taught her to fend for herself, and released her back into her natural habitat. Elsa was the first lioness ever successfully released into the wild. She went on to have a litter of cubs, but sadly, Elsa died from a tick bite at age five.

In 1960, Joy wrote a book called *Born Free*. It was about her work with African lions in general, and with Elsa in particular. It became an international bestseller and, in 1966, it was made into a movie.

With her book, Joy became the first person to raise awareness of the plight of endangered animals in Africa. Not everyone appreciated her work, though—Joy was murdered by poachers in 1980.

For Dian, though, living in the jungle with mountain gorillas was exactly where she wanted to be. The gentle, playful gorillas were the family she'd never had. They accepted her into their midst, allowing her to observe them at close range. She befriended these gentle giants. She communicated with them. She also did whatever she had to do to protect them.

In the end, Dian's passion for her beloved mountain gorillas would be her downfall— perhaps not a surprising outcome for someone who, even as a child, was more at ease with animals than with her own species.

Dian and a baby gorilla at ease with one another in the forest.

Chapter 2
Lifelong Animal Lover

Dian looks on as photographer Liam White makes friends with a baby gorilla at Dian's research camp in Africa.

Dian Fossey was born in San Francisco, California, on January 16, 1932. She was the only child of Kitty, a fashion model, and George, an insurance salesman. George loved his daughter, but didn't enjoy his life. As a result, he drank excessively and often got into trouble with the police. Because of the problems associated with George's drinking and other difficulties, Dian's parents divorced when she was six. A year later, Kitty married a wealthy businessman named Richard Price. Neither he nor Kitty paid much attention to Dian, who grew up as a shy, unhappy, lonely little girl.

Finding Friendship with Animals

To ease her loneliness, Dian longed for a pet. The only animal her parents allowed in the house, though, was a goldfish. When the fish died, "I cried for a week," said Dian. "My parents thought it good riddance, so I never got another."

Fortunately, Kitty and Richard allowed Dian to ride horses. This was the one joy in the little girl's life. When she was in high school, she joined the riding team, where she excelled.

Otherwise, Dian did not enjoy her teenage years. By age 14, she was more than six feet (182 centimeters) tall. She towered over

Dian stands tall among other members of her high school graduating class in this photo, taken in 1949.

her classmates. She felt awkward and ugly, feelings that pushed her to isolate herself even further. Even her mother, who was once called "the most beautiful model in the city" of San Francisco, thought her daughter unattractive and ungainly. Dian's stepfather simply ignored the girl.

It's no wonder that, by this time, Dian was already more comfortable with animals than she was with people.

After she graduated from high school, 17-year-old Dian followed her stepfather's wishes and enrolled in business courses at Marin Junior College in Kentfield, California. Even though her parents were wealthy, they didn't support her financially. Dian worked as a clerk at a department store to cover her costs of living. Her heart wasn't in the job, and she hated business school. Luckily, after her first year at Marin, Dian's love of animals pointed her in a new direction.

Two photos of Dian from her 1949 senior yearbook at Lowell High School in San Francisco. One of them is her class picture, the other a photo taken of students involved in school activities.

FIELD NOTES

Many famous people attended Marin Junior College (or the College of Marin, as it is now called). Voice actor Jack Angel, whose voice has been featured in such animated films as *Monsters Inc.*, *Cars*, *Horton Hears a Who*, and *A Bug's Life*, attended the school. Singer-songwriter Naomi Judd is also a Marin grad, as is NFL player Honor Jackson. The most famous person to attend the College of Marin was actor and comedian Robin Williams.

In the summer of 1950, Dian's passion for horses, and her experience as a rider, landed her a job at a dude ranch in Montana. That's a place where tourists go to ride horses and live like cowboys and cowgirls during their vacations. At the ranch, Dian spent her days with horses and other farm animals. She loved every minute of it!

For the first time in years, she was happy. It was "the best job I'd ever had," she said. Unfortunately, Dian came down with chicken pox and had to leave the job before the summer was over. By the time she left Montana, though, her future was clear—she knew she wanted to work with animals.

Two photos from Dian's senior year in high school reflect her involvement with horses as a teenager. Top: dressed in her horse-riding gear, with other leaders of the Girls' Athletic Association. Bottom: on her high school riding team (right).

Immediately, Dian enrolled in a pre-veterinary program at the University of California, Davis. She excelled in most of her courses, but she struggled with chemistry and physics. She worked hard for two years. In the end, however, her science grades simply weren't strong enough for her to continue on in veterinary studies. Once again, Dian was forced to change career paths.

This time, she chose to study occupational therapy at San Jose State College. She decided that, if she couldn't work with animals, she would work with disabled children. Dian graduated with a degree in occupational therapy in 1954 at the age of 22.

DIAN'S OCCUPATION

When Dian earned her degree in Occupational Therapy (OT), it was a fairly new field. Today, OT is commonly practiced in hospitals, seniors' homes, homeless shelters, schools, and many other social and health-care facilities.

Occupational therapists help people learn or adjust activities to enrich their lives. Many OT patients are recovering from injury, dealing with the conditions of aging, or undergoing a major lifestyle change. In these cases, people may have to relearn activities that were once easy for them. This is where the OT comes in.

Occupational therapists also work with adults and children with disabilities, troubled or at-risk youths who need to learn to function in society in a healthy way, and even stressed-out executives. The goal of OT is to help people live happy, healthy, productive lives by improving the "occupations," or activities, of day-to-day life.

A Love of Children and Animals

To become a registered occupational therapist, Dian had to intern, or work under the direction of others who are more experienced. For nine months, she worked at a variety of hospitals near her parents' home in California.

As soon as she was certified and ready to work full time, she moved as far from her mother and stepfather as she could get. She took a job at Kosair Crippled Children's Hospital in Louisville, Kentucky—2,300 miles (3,700 kilometers) away. Another reason she chose this particular hospital was because, in Louisville, she could pursue her passion for animals. Kentucky was horse country!

Kosair was a small hospital in a setting that was both suburban and rustic. Many of the young patients had polio, a viral disease that can lead to muscle weakness, especially in the legs. Some polio patients lose the ability to walk. Today, thanks to widespread vaccination against the disease, polio has been nearly wiped out. In 1955, when Dian started at Kosair, the

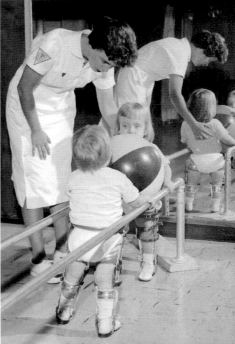

A physical therapist works with two young children with polio as they exercise their legs. In the 1950s and 1960s, which is when this photo was taken, the exciting, groundbreaking development of anti-polio vaccines immunized thousands of people who might otherwise have contracted the disease. Still, many people had contracted the disease before the vaccines were available to them, and they needed physical and occupational therapy from workers like Dian to help strengthen their bodies.

vaccine to prevent polio was not quite ready for public use. There is no known "cure" for polio. So even when the vaccine became available in the mid to late 1950s, most people who had contracted the virus in years past would live with the effects of polio for the rest of their lives. They needed physical therapy and other kinds of medical support.

Dian also worked with children with autism. These kids often had trouble communicating with others. "These children have a variety of physical and emotional disabilities and are lost in this world of ours," she wrote. "They need a tremendous amount of care and kindness to make them feel life is worth living."

Dian was a compassionate, kind, and respectful caregiver, but she also pushed the children to work hard. Her tough-love approach didn't suit every child, but most of them responded to her way of working.

Dian loved the children in her care. She felt the same sort of kinship with them that she felt with animals—one she didn't share with adults.

Dian rarely socialized with her Kosair coworkers, and she lived in an isolated cottage on a farm outside the city limits. There, she helped with the farmer's cattle and took in a variety of stray animals. Three farm dogs, named Mitzi, Shep, and Brownie, "adopted me as one of their own," she said.

In all her years at Kosair, Dian only made one good friend, a young woman named Mary Henry. Mary realized Dian was shy and lacking confidence, not snobby and strange as some of her colleagues believed.

Gradually, the two young women got to

know each other, until one day, Mary invited Dian home for lunch. After that, Dian became a regular guest at the Henry home. For the first time, she felt a connection to a family, something she had never experienced with her own parents.

Mary and her family were wealthy and well connected in Louisville society. Through them, Dian met all sorts of fascinating folks, including a number of people who had traveled to Africa. Their stories instantly grabbed Dian's attention. "The thought of being where the animals haven't all been driven into little corners attracts me so much," she wrote at the time.

Dian's interest in Africa was further fueled in 1960, when Mary went to visit friends in Rhodesia (now Zimbabwe). Mary also went on a safari during her stay in the southeastern African nation. Mary had asked Dian to join her on the trip, but, as much as she wanted to go, Dian could not afford such an adventure.

When Mary returned, she shared her stories and photographs of Africa with her friend. Dian was so inspired by what she saw and heard that she decided that somehow, some day, she would find a way to go to Africa.

A Dream Come True

For three years, Dian planned every detail of a trip she hoped to take to Africa. She studied maps and took lessons in Swahili, a common language in parts of Africa. She got all the immunization shots she would need. She bought safari clothes, rugged boots, and bug spray. She read everything she could find about Africa and its animals.

FIELD NOTES

Little was known by Westerners about mountain gorillas in the mid 20th century, because they had first been seen by non-native people only 50 years earlier. It was dangerous and expensive to venture to their habitat to study them, so few Westerners had done so.

The towering volcanic peak of Mount Nyiragongo in the Virunga Mountains, which are home to the mountain gorillas of central Africa. The name "Virunga" is an English version of a word in the Kinyarwanda language that means "volcano." Nyiragongo, which is located in Virunga National Park in the Democratic Republic of the Congo is an active volcano.

Dian was most fascinated by a book called *The Year of the Gorilla,* by American zoologist George Schaller. He was the first person to study the rare mountain gorillas. Upon reading his book, Dian decided her African adventure must include a visit to the mountain gorillas' home—the Virunga Mountains in the center of the continent.

By early 1963, Dian was ready to take her dream trip—except for one thing. She still had no money, and she knew the journey would cost a fortune.

Because it would be the trip of a lifetime for her, she intended to spare no expense. She would make sure she saw everything she wanted to see and did everything she wanted to do in Africa. That meant the trip would cost the equivalent of a year and a half of her Kosair salary.

Dian's parents would not lend her money for an expedition they considered dangerous. An aunt and uncle, who had helped her financially when she was a university student, also refused to support her adventure. "It's madness," they told her. "If you had any sense, you'd call the whole thing off."

But Dian had no intention of letting a lack of funds keep her from realizing her dream. She knew she would find a way to pay for her African adventure.

She began approaching banks, asking for a loan. She was refused time and time again.

Finally, Dian found a bank that would lend her money—at an outrageous interest rate. She borrowed $8,000 against her future earnings. "I committed myself to a three-year bank debt in order to finance a seven-week safari," she wrote.

With everything in place, on September 26, 1963, Dian flew to Nairobi, Kenya—with 60 pounds (27 kilograms) of luggage.

Once there, she met up with John Alexander, a British hunter she had hired, by mail, from her home in Louisville. John was to be her personal guide through Africa. Their route would take them through a number of national parks and game preserves in Kenya, Tanganyika (now Tanzania), Uganda, and Congo. After that, Dian would continue on by

herself, to visit Mary Henry's friends in Rhodesia.

Almost as soon as Dian and John took to the road in Kenya, they began to see the wildlife Dian had dreamed of viewing. Over the next few weeks, she saw hundreds of wild animals—rhinos, elephants, giraffes, lions, and "herds of wildebeest, zebra, impala," she wrote.

On the famous Serengeti Plains in Tanzania, Dian and John stopped at Olduvai Gorge. World-famous archaeologist and paleontologist Louis Leakey had been digging for fossils there for more than 30 years. Dian knew of his work and of his support for Jane Goodall's study of chimpanzees. She also knew that the chances of meeting Louis were slim.

During her trip to Africa in 1963, Dian visited many places that fueled her passion for the continent's incredible assortment of wildlife. Among the stops on her tour were the following sites:

Top: The Tsavo Conservation Area, which is home to Kenya's largest elephant population.

Middle: Lake Manyara in Tanzania, with its huge assortment of pelicans and flamingoes.

Bottom: The Ngorongoro Conservation Area in Tanzania, named after its huge, 12.5-mile- (20-km-) wide volcanic crater. Shown here are wildebeests, zebras, and flamingoes, with the sides of the crater in the background.

By that time, Louis was 60 years old and spending most of his time in the city of Nairobi, rather than at the dig site.

Remarkably, on the day Dian visited Olduvai Gorge, he was there! Even better, he spent several minutes talking to her about where she'd been in Africa, what she planned to see next, and her interest in mountain gorillas. Louis also arranged for Dian to tour archaeological sites.

"THE CHIMP GIRL"

Jane Goodall was born in London, England, in 1934. When she was 23 years old, she met Louis Leakey during a visit to Africa and became his assistant. When Louis was ready to launch a long-term study of chimpanzees, he hired Jane as the researcher. In July 1960, Jane began her study at the Gombe Stream Chimpanzee Reserve in western Tanganyika (which became Tanzania four years later.)

In the 26 years she spent at Gombe, Jane made a number of important discoveries. She found that chimps were not strictly vegetarians as previously believed. They do eat meat. She also discovered that the animals could make and use tools, and that they share more in common with humans than previously known. Like people, they have emotions, intelligence, and individual personalities. They can also be violent toward each other, as can human beings.

In 1977, Jane founded the Jane Goodall Institute, a global organization dedicated to wildlife conservation and habitat preservation. Now in her 80s, Jane continues to devote her life to educating the public about the threats facing chimpanzees in particular, and the environment in general.

Jane Goodall, photographed with a chimpanzee around 1965.

During her tour of Olduvai Gorge, Dian slipped and twisted her ankle. That might have prevented some people from continuing to trek through Africa, but Dian wasn't about to let a sprained ankle keep her from viewing the mountain gorillas she had come to see.

She said goodbye to Louis Leakey and his wife Mary, and continued on to a village called Kisoro, about 1,000 miles (1,600 km) to the northwest. Kisoro is located in Uganda on the western slopes of the Virunga Mountains.

On October 16, 1963, Dian and John, along with two armed rangers and 11 porters to carry their gear, set out to climb Mount Mikeno, in the Congo section of the Virungas—into mountain gorilla territory.

Despite her swollen ankle, Dian made the climb up to the Kabara Meadow, also in Congo,

"It took six-and-a-half hours to get to this camp, and I thought I would die. My rib cage was bursting, my legs were creaking and in agony, and my ankle felt as though a crocodile had his jaws around it."

Dian Fossey, on her trek up Mount Mikeno

Mount Mikeno, on the Congo side of the Virunga Mountains, looms above a ranger station in Virunga National Park.

where a pair of photographers, Joan and Alan Root, had set up camp.

The photographers had been there for several weeks, filming gorillas. At first, they were annoyed that Dian and her group had disturbed their work. They ignored Dian and her guides, who spent a few days searching for—but not finding—gorillas. Eventually, the Roots "took pity on me and asked if I wanted to go out with them" as they photographed the great apes, said Dian. Of course, she took them up on their offer!

The Roots and their local trackers knew exactly how and where to find gorillas. They took the lead and guided Dian's group into the mountains. "The terrain was unbelievable, almost straight up," wrote Dian, a heavy smoker who struggled to breathe in the thin mountain air. Eventually, the hikers came across a space where a group of gorillas had clearly spent the previous night.

Almost immediately, they detected an odor, "an overwhelming, musky, barnyard yet humanlike stench," wrote Dian. "Then the thin mountain air was shattered like window glass by a high-pitched series of deafening screams."

The only thing that prevented her from running away, she said, was that she was blocked by the guide standing behind her. "For a minute, the chill, fog-dripping forest was unbelievably silent," she continued. "Then it was rent by even more ferocious screams punctuated by thunderous drumlike tattoos."

The group froze until the screaming and pounding stopped. Silently, one of the local trackers, a man named Sanweke, cut "a

A silverback, or mature male mountain gorilla, beats his chest as his picture is taken at a national park. Silverbacks use this kind of aggressive behavior, known as displaying, when they are protecting their families or confronting other males, often during mating competitions. Such displays include hooting, charging from side to side, slapping and tearing vegetation, chest beating with cupped hands, and thumping the ground with their hands to end the display. It was this kind of drumming noise that Dian heard when she ventured out with photographers Joan and Alan Root.

window" through the thick jungle foliage. Alan Root motioned for Dian to step forward. Dian wrote about what she saw next:

"I peered through the opening. There they were: the devilmen of native stories; the basis of the King Kong myth; the last of the Mountain Kings of Africa.
A group of about six adult gorillas stared apprehensively back at us through the opening in the wall of vegetation.... They were big and imposing but not monstrous at all. Somehow they looked more like members of a picnic party surprised by interlopers [intruders]. Their bright gazes darted nervously from under their brows as they tried to determine if we were dangerous."

In this publicity still from the 1933 movie King Kong, *Kong terrorizes his female captive and battles planes from the top of the Empire State Building in New York City. Released less than 100 years after the first scientific proof of the existence of gorillas, the movie took full advantage of people's most extreme fears and fantasies about our close genetic relations!*

A family of mountain gorillas (the silverback is far right, the female far left) upon being photographed near their home in the Virunga Mountains.

31

GORILLAS GET A BAD RAP

In 1847, the *Boston Journal of Natural History* published photographs of the skull of a never-before-seen animal. The pair of Americans who discovered the skull called the new animal *Troglodytes gorills*, after the name given, by an ancient explorer, to a tribe of wild, hairy women.

For centuries, there had been rumors that hairy, human-like beasts lived in the jungles of Africa. Some adventurers had even claimed to have seen them. They described these half-man, half-beasts as evil flesh-eaters who particularly enjoyed devouring women.

The 1847 skull discovery provided the first scientific proof that a large, human-like animal actually existed.

In the 1850s and 1860s, a French explorer named Paul du Chaillu spent several years traveling around Africa. During his expeditions, he observed gorillas in the wild. He also killed several, delivering their dead bodies to museums in America and Europe. Paul wrote stories about the gorillas, describing them as ferocious, bloodthirsty beasts. These stories furthered the public's fear of—and fascination with—the mysterious creatures.

In 1887, a French artist won a prestigious prize for his sculpture called *Gorilla Carrying Off a Woman* (shown here). This statue of a fierce gorilla holding a limp, helpless woman became internationally famous and reinforced the belief that gorillas were savage monsters.

In 1902, a German army officer was the first non-native person to spot a new species of gorilla. In the Virunga Mountains, where Dian Fossey later conducted her studies, he saw what would come to be called mountain gorillas. He killed two and took them to a museum in Germany.

In the early 20th century, wicked gorillas became trendy as characters in books, films, plays, comics, and children's literature. The nastiest gorilla of all made his film debut in 1933 as the title character in *King Kong*. The movie sealed the gorillas' bloodthirsty image once and for all—or at least until zoologist George Schaller came along. It was when George began his studies of mountain gorillas in 1959 that the world realized these great apes weren't so bad after all.

Dian managed to snap a few photographs of the shy creatures before she and her colleagues backed away. Quietly, they retreated, leaving the gorillas in peace.

It was a life-changing moment for Dian—her dream of seeing these magnificent animals had come true! "I left with reluctance," she wrote, "but with never a doubt that I would, somehow, return to learn more about the gorillas of the misted mountains."

"Immediately I was struck by the physical magnificence of the huge jet-black bodies blended against the green palette wash of the thick forest foliage."

Dian's first impression of mountain gorillas

Chapter 3
Into Africa

U pon her return from Africa, Dian Fossey went back to her job at Kosair Crippled Children's Hospital in Louisville. She worked there for three more years, earning the money she needed to repay the loan she had taken for her African adventure. More than half of each paycheck went to repaying her debt. During this time, Dian also wrote a number of articles for her local newspaper about her encounter with the mountain gorillas. The photographs that accompanied her articles—the ones she had taken high in the mountains of Africa—would soon change her life.

A baby gorilla inside Virunga National Park.

Preparing for the Role of a Lifetime

On April 3, 1966, Louis Leakey came to Louisville to present his lecture about his archaeological work and interest in primates. Dian was fascinated by his theories about the connections between great apes and the evolution of humankind.

After Louis's three-hour lecture, Dian joined a long line of admirers who waited to speak to the famous scientist. She hoped he would remember meeting her in Africa three years earlier. When she got to the front of the line, she was thrilled to discover that not only did he remember her, but he also asked about her sprained ankle!

Today we know much more about mountain gorillas than when Dian first set out to study them. It's easy to find photos like these in books and online, but when Dian took her pictures, mountain gorillas were still somewhat mysterious creatures that few people had seen. Shots like these of female mountain gorillas and their babies caused quite a sensation!

"I was so surprised he knew me that I just pushed my damp and wrinkled articles into his hand," she wrote. While Louis wasn't particularly interested in the articles she'd written, the accompanying photographs caught his attention. He asked Dian to wait until everyone else had left the lecture hall, so he could speak to her privately. She later wrote:

"Not knowing what to expect, I waited at the back of the stage, until finally he came over and started throwing a barrage of questions at me…. I told him that all I really wanted was to spend my life working with animals— that had always been my dream, and I was especially interested in the gorillas on the Virunga Mountains."

Louis was impressed with the young woman's passion and determination. "You might be just the person I have in mind to start a long-term study of gorillas," he said. He asked Dian to meet him the following morning.

Dian couldn't believe it. "Things just don't happen like this," she wrote in her journal.

The hour-long meeting did happen, though, and Louis did ask her if she would be interested in conducting the gorilla study he was proposing. It was here that he asked her to become "the gorilla girl."

Of course, she accepted his offer!

Two months later, Dian quit her job at Kosair Hospital, where she had worked for 11 years. "Leaving the place I'd grown to love—the children, my home, the farm dogs, and my friends—was one of the most difficult things I've ever had to do," she wrote.

She packed up her things and drove to California to spend time with her parents before she left the country. Her mother and stepfather were horrified by Dian's decision. They could not understand why a 34-year-old woman would want to live alone in the jungles of Africa.

It would be another six months before Louis organized the funding and permits necessary for Dian to study the gorillas in Africa. During that time, she continued to study Swahili, and she took a university course in primatology (the study of primates). She read and re-read George Schaller's three books on mountain gorillas.

Finally, on December 15, 1966, with finances and permits in place, Dian boarded a plane to Africa. With her, she took her typewriter, four cameras, office supplies, and three years' worth of sturdy clothing.

FIELD NOTES

Louis Leakey had interviewed 22 other potential researchers before he hired Dian to conduct the mountain gorilla study.

"There was no way I could explain to dogs, friends or parents my compelling need to return to Africa to launch a long-term study of the gorillas."

Dian Fossey, *Gorillas in the Mist*

THE GORILLA MAN BEFORE DIAN

Dian Fossey's passion for mountain gorillas was inspired by American zoologist George Schaller and his book *The Year of the Gorilla*. Beginning in 1959, George spent a year conducting a behavioral study of mountain gorillas in Albert National Park (later renamed Virunga National Park) in central Africa. He set up his camp at Kabara, on the slopes of Mount Mikeno—the same place Dian set up her first camp eight years later. Dian would later meet some of the same gorillas George had studied and written about.

George was the first person to conduct a long-term study of mountain gorillas. He discovered they were intelligent and gentle animals, not the King Kong-like monsters many people believed they were. He spent more than 450 hours observing gorillas in the Virunga Mountains. Like Dian's study, his was cut short because of political turmoil in the area.

George wrote three books about mountain gorillas and his experiences with them. He was considered "the" expert on the animals until Dian came along.

Now in his 80s, George is vice-president of Panthera, an organization dedicated to the conservation of the world's wild cats. He is one of the planet's most important wildlife biologists, having studied endangered animals in Africa, Asia, and South America.

American zoologist George Schaller is photographed while studying gorillas in Africa in 1963.

A Dream Come True

On her way to Kenya, Dian had a stopover in London. Coincidentally, photographer Joan Root was there at exactly the same time. Three years after they'd first met, the two women ran into each other in the airport. This turned out to be a lucky break for Dian!

Joan was shocked to learn that Dian was about to head into the African jungle by herself. She knew Dian wasn't prepared for the mission she was about to undertake. Dian didn't speak local languages, she had weak lungs from a lifetime of smoking, and she knew nothing about the customs of the local people. She certainly did not understand the political turmoil raging in the region at that time.

When they landed in Nairobi, Kenya, Joan insisted that her husband Alan accompany Dian on the 700-mile (1,100-km) drive to the Virunga Mountains.

Before they departed, Louis Leakey bought Dian an old canvas-topped Land Rover. Dian named it "Lily." Joan helped her buy all the food and supplies she would need to set up her research camp.

Dian spent Christmas 1966 near Nairobi, with Jane Goodall, "the chimp girl," as Dian called her. The two women then flew 800 miles (1,300 km) southwest to Jane's research station in the far west of Tanzania (formerly Tanganyika). The plan was for Dian to spend 10 days there, learning research techniques from Jane before she started her own study. In the end, because of schedules and delays, Dian only spent two days with Jane before returning to Nairobi.

Early in January, with Lily packed to the roof, Dian set out on the long drive to the Virunga Mountains. Alan Root, in his own Land Rover, led the way. After four days, the two vehicles arrived at the village of Kisoro, at the junction of the Rwanda, Uganda, and Congo borders. There, a friend of Alan's warned them to steer clear of Congo. The political unrest in that nation made it a dangerous place for foreigners, particularly white foreigners, he said.

Despite the risks, Dian refused to delay her gorilla research. Alan helped her get the necessary permits, pass through police barricades, and cross the border into Congo. At the base of Mount Mikeno, Dian hired a pair of armed guards and about two dozen porters to help carry her gear up the mountain.

Her plan was to set up camp in the Kabara Meadow, where Alan and Joan were based when she had first met them. Dian expected to stay there for at least two years, getting to know the local gorilla population.

Like the previous time she'd climbed Mount Mikeno, Dian struggled with this uphill trek.

Wildlife photographer Joan Root is shown offering a grasshopper treat to a red-billed hornbill in Tsavo National Park, Kenya. With her husband Alan, who was also a photographer, Joan helped Dian through some challenging times when Dian settled into her life in the wild.

"The heaviness of limb and shortness of breath that come with the altitude were vividly familiar," she wrote.

At the top, though, her efforts were rewarded. "When we reached the Kabara meadow, we saw that it had remained unspoiled," she said. "In fact, it seemed scarcely to have changed at all in the three years since I'd last been there."

Alan spent two days with Dian helping her establish her research camp. When he left, on January 15, 1967, she realized how alone she was. "I'll never forget the feeling of sheer panic that I felt watching him depart," she wrote in her journal. "He was my last contact with

PRESERVING PARKS

In the early 20th century, what is now the nation known as the Democratic Republic of the Congo was governed by Belgium and called the Belgian Congo. In 1925, the Belgian government established Albert National Park, the first national park in Africa. It was named after King Albert of Belgium. At the time, most of the park was in the Belgian Congo, but it included a tiny piece of land in northwestern Rwanda. This small area, which included Mount Visoke and Mount Karisimbi, was home to mountain gorillas.

In 1960, the Congo and Rwanda sides of the park were divided into two separate protected areas. The tiny Rwanda side of the park, where Dian would later work, was named Volcanoes National Park. The Congo part of the park, where Dian set up her first research camp, was called Albert Park until 1969. That year, it was renamed Virunga National Park.

civilization as I had known it. I found myself clinging to the tent pole simply to avoid running after him."

For four days, Dian was alone in the jungle with a pair of local helpers whose language she did not speak. On January 19, her fears somewhat subsided when Sanweke arrived. He was the tracker she had met on her first trip to the area, and he would become her trusted companion for years to come.

Dian's First Home Away from Home

A present-day tracker in the Virunga Mountains helps a researcher examine droppings and other evidence of gorilla activity as they make their way to a nearby mountain gorilla community.

A Guide and Good Friend

On her first trip to Africa, Dian Fossey met a Congolese tracker named Sanweke (also spelled "Sanwekwe"). At the time, he was a tracker and guide for photographers Joan and Alan Root. In 1960, Sanweke had also worked with George Schaller, whose books had inspired Dian's interest in gorillas.

Sanweke was a brilliant tracker, who taught Dian all the tricks and techniques she needed to locate mountain gorillas on her own. He helped her survive in the Virunga Mountains, especially during her early years there. He was to become her lifelong friend and trusted companion.

The day Sanweke arrived, he and Dian went tracking—and found a group of nine gorillas! Dian labeled this family Group 1. Before long, she too became a talented tracker and often went out on her own to observe the animals' behavior. During the next few months, Dian identified and focused her studies on three distinct gorilla groups. She called them simply Group 1, Group 2, and Group 3.

At first, she kept her distance from the majestic creatures. She watched them through binoculars, making sure she didn't scare them. After about two months, though, she discovered that she could gain their trust by mimicking their behavior. She became one of them!

She began grunting and burping and making other gorilla sounds. She started to knuckle walk, groom herself, and eat wild celery the way they did. The gorillas were as curious about Dian as she was about them. She wrote about it in her journal:

"To be perfectly frank, I think they are quite confused as to my species! I've been following one gorilla group around all month, and now I'm able to get within 30 to 60 feet [10–20 meters] of them and they are not afraid of me. To be perfectly frank, I think they are quite confused as to my species!... [T]hey are fascinated by my facial grimaces and other actions that I wouldn't be caught dead doing in front of anyone. I feel like a complete fool, but this technique seems to be working.... Last week, two of them approached me

to within 20 feet [6 m].... There aren't words to describe what a thrill that was, and as long as I live, I'll never forget it."
Gradually, Dian was able to identify individuals within

This photo shows Dian and a mountain gorilla with whom she has gained enough trust to get close to and sit with. Over the course of her life and work with the gorillas, Dian was careful to allow the gorillas to determine the kind of "space" they would occupy with her.

each family group. She realized that each one had a distinct personality and a distinct nose print, a pattern of lines on its nose. She drew diagrams of the nose prints and gave the gorillas names to help keep them straight in her journals. She called them such things as Solomon, No-nose, Hugger, Popcorn, and Monarch. She also named some of them after friends and family members back home.

Dian kept detailed records of her gorilla research, with charts, graphs, drawings, analysis, and written observations. She spent evenings in her tent typing up her notes. If she had time, she also recorded observations about local plants, the weather, and other wildlife. "It was always a most delightful, cozy feeling to type up field notes near the crackling fireplace at night with the sounds of the owls, hyrax, antelope, buffalo, and elephants outside," she wrote.

For more than six months, Dian lived on

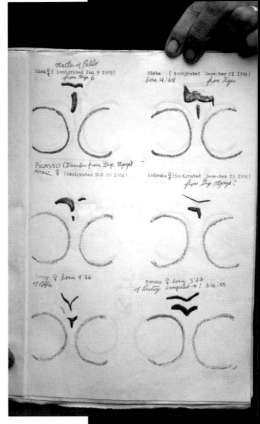

These records made by Dian include diagrams she drew of nose prints and other details of the gorillas she studied and became close to.

Field Notes

At Kabara Meadow camp, on the slopes of Mount Mikeno in Congo, Dian lived in a seven-by-ten-foot (two-by-three-meter) tent that served as her bedroom, office, laundry room, and bathroom. She prepared her meals in a separate wooden shack. Once a month, she hiked down the mountain to where her Land Rover, Lily, was parked and drove two hours to a nearby village to buy food.

Mount Mikeno, studying gorillas, writing up her research, photographing and sketching the apes.

During this time, the gorillas got used to Dian's presence. Only once, when she and Sanweke accidentally startled a pair, did they become aggressive. "It wasn't a bluff charge—they really meant it," she wrote. She and Sanweke ran and barely escaped. "When their long, yellow canines [teeth] and wild eyes were no less than two feet away, I took a very ungainly nosedive into the thick foliage alongside the trail. They whizzed on by, caught up in their own momentum."

MOUNTAIN GORILLAS 101

One of the first things Dian learned about gorillas at Kabara was that she couldn't just sit and watch them. That made them uncomfortable, so they didn't act naturally. For Dian to witness "real" behavior, the gorillas had to accept her into their midst. By imitating their feeding and grooming behavior, their body language and their sounds, she earned their trust. She also learned that gorillas startle easily, so she always moved slowly around them.

She discovered that each gorilla family group has one leader, a mature male, at least 15 years old. He is called a silverback because his coat is turning gray. Each group also contains one younger male, aged 8 to 13, called a blackback. The rest of the group is made up of mature females, which mate with the silverback, and younger gorillas, labeled "young adults, "juveniles," or "infants," depending on their size.

In the evenings, gorilla families sleep in nests made of twigs and leaves. During the daytime, they roam, feed, and rest on a regular schedule.

Adult gorillas are patient with their young, letting the little ones jump on them, pull their hair, and romp around them. The adults are also affectionate, and they cuddle their young.

In general, Dian discovered, gorillas are gentle beasts that only become violent when threatened. Their only enemies are the humans who hunt them. Gorillas will fight to the death to protect their families.

It was during her months at Kabara that Dian began what would become a lifelong hatred of poachers. Poachers are people who illegally hunt and kill wildlife. Dian's first encounter with poachers happened in March 1967. While tracking gorillas, she and Sanweke stumbled upon an armed group of poachers. Dian seized their spears, while Sanweke pointed a gun at them. The plan was to march them down the mountain and hand them over to authorities, but the poachers managed to escape.

As it turned out, the poachers weren't Dian's only problem.

A silverback and his baby play while relaxing with other family members in Volcanoes National Park. Mountain gorillas are normally gentle creatures, but they will fight fiercely to defend their families.

What she didn't realize, because she was so isolated on Mount Mikeno, was that the political situation in Congo was, by now, in chaos—and the president considered white people the enemy.

In her book *Gorillas in the Mist*, which she wrote many years later, Dian describes how one evening early in July, she was shocked to find a group of armed guards waiting for her at Kabara. They demolished her camp, escorted her off the mountain, and held her captive for two weeks. In the book she hints that she was abused while being kept prisoner. Using her wits and her money to bribe guards, she finally managed to escape into Uganda.

At the time these events occurred, however, Dian told a different version of the story. In letters and sworn statements, she said government officials insisted that, for her own safety, she abandon Kabara. She didn't like the idea, but she agreed to pack up and leave. Guards escorted her to the national park office, where she spent a week waiting for the turmoil to settle down.

She also said at the time that, after dealing with obnoxious officials, pushy customs officers, and threats of imprisonment (because Lily wasn't properly registered), she drove back to Mount Mikeno, intent on returning to her research camp. Local guards, however, would not allow her back onto the mountain—and by this time, the border to Uganda was closed. After waiting another week at the base of the mountain, Dian gave up, bribed a border guard, and crossed into Uganda.

Whichever version of the story is true, the result was that Dian never returned to Kabara.

CHAOS IN CONGO

Dian Fossey arrived in Congo at one of the most turbulent times in the country's history. After being under Belgian rule for decades, Congo became an independent republic in 1960. Unfortunately, nobody had a plan for the country after Belgium handed it over. For the next five years, the country endured uprisings and civil war as different leaders fought for the right to rule the nation.

In November 1965, a man named Mobutu Sese Seko took power. He didn't trust the Congolese army. He thought soldiers might try to overthrow him. To keep them under control, he brought in a group of white mercenaries, or highly trained professional soldiers.

On July 5, 1967, while Dian was at work at Kabara, the mercenaries turned on both the president and the Congolese Army and massacred many people. Immediately, President Mobutu declared all white people the enemy. He declared a state of emergency in Congo and closed the borders.

Dian was one of the white people detained by the Congolese army, until she escaped into Uganda.

Mobutu Sese Seko was military dictator and president of the Democratic Republic of the Congo from 1965 to 1997. In 1971, he renamed the country Zaire, a name that stood until he was overthrown and fled the country. During his time in office he gathered huge personal wealth and political power. Most of it came through corrupt financial dealings and brutal practices against all those he saw as his enemies, Congolese and foreigners alike.

Instead, she traveled from Uganda to Nairobi, Kenya, to meet with Louis Leakey.

A New Start in a New Home

Despite the danger, and against the advice of the United States Embassy, Dian and Louis Leakey decided she would continue her work with mountain gorillas. This time, though, she would set up a new camp, on the Rwandan side of the Virunga Mountains.

While she was in Nairobi with Louis, Dian met a woman who would become a friend for life—Alyette de Munck, a wealthy explorer and naturalist. Alyette owned a plantation on the Rwanda side of the Virunga Mountains, in the foothills of Mount Karisimbi. Reeling from personal tragedies involving the unexpected death of her husband and then, several months later, the killing of her son by members of the Congolese military, Alyette threw herself into helping Dian establish a new gorilla research station.

Together, in September 1967, the two women set up Dian's new camp in the valley between

A village at the base of Mount Visoke (shown in the background) in Volcanoes National Park, on the Rwanda side of the Virunga Mountains. This is the area where Dian set up a new camp after abandoning Kabara, which had become off-limits in the wake of political strife in Congo.

two mountains—Mount Karisimbi and Mount Visoke (also called "Bisoke"). Dian combined the mountains' names and called her facility the Karisoke Research Center. It was located just three miles (five km)—across a valley and the border—from Kabara.

"Little did I know then that by setting up two small tents in the wilderness of the Virungas, I had launched the beginnings of what was to become an internationally renowned research station," wrote Dian in her book *Gorillas in the Mist*.

Karisoke would be Dian's home for the rest of her life.

What's in a Name?

Around the time Dian lived in Africa, the region was seething with political turmoil. Because of this, many of the countries she visited changed names many times over the years. To help clear up confusion about which country was which, and what it became later, here's a helpful chart. The names in the left column are what the countries were called when Dian visited them.

The maps on the opposite page show these and other African nations named in this book in relation to one another and to all of Africa. The names and borders are the countries' current ones.

COUNTRIES DIAN VISITED	OFFICIAL NAMES
Congo	Congo Free State (1885–1908)
	Belgian Congo (1908–1960)
	Republic of Congo (1960–1965)
	Democratic Republic of the Congo (1965–1971)
	Republic of Zaire (1971–1997)
	Democratic Republic of the Congo (1997–present)
Kenya	Kenya (1920–1964)
	Republic of Kenya (1964–present)
Rhodesia	Southern Rhodesia (1898–1964)
	Rhodesia (1964–1970)
	Republic of Rhodesia (1970–May 1979)
	Zimbabwe Rhodesia (May 1979–April 1980)
	Republic of Zimbabwe (April 1980–present)
Rwanda	Kingdom of Rwanda (15th century–1962)
	Republic of Rwanda (1962–present)
Tanganyika/Tanzania	Tanganyika (1916–1961)
	Republic of Tanganyika (1962–1964)
	United Republic of Tanzania (1964–present)
Uganda	Uganda (1894–1962)
	Republic of Uganda (1962–present)

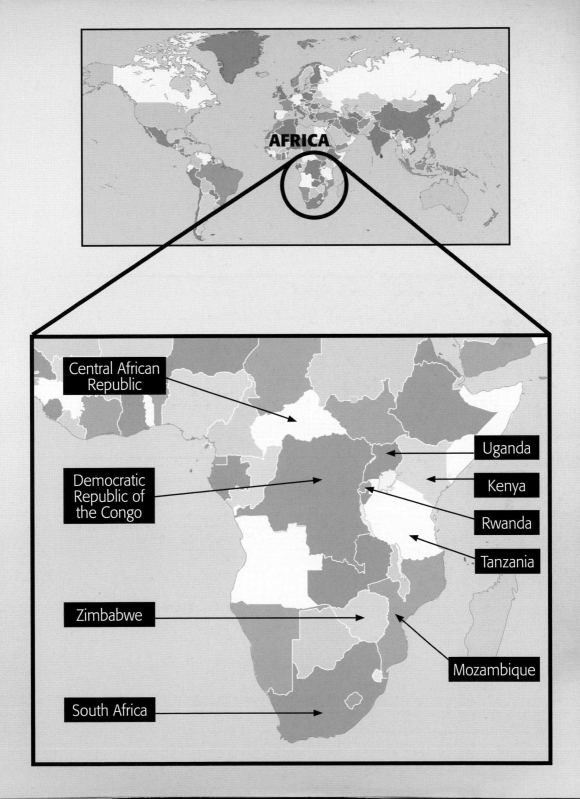

AFRICA

Central African
Republic

Uganda

Kenya

Democratic
Republic of
the Congo

Rwanda

Tanzania

Zimbabwe

Mozambique

South Africa

Chapter 4
Nyiramachabelli *

The first time Dian Fossey visited Africa, she'd met a young man named Alexie Forrester. At the time, he lived in Rhodesia (present-day Zimbabwe). Now, four years later, he was a student in the United States. Since they'd met, Dian and Alexie had been involved in an on-again, off-again relationship, depending on where each of them was living. In September 1967, shortly after Dian set up her camp at Karisoke, her worried parents sent Alexie to Africa to bring their daughter home. He showed up with an engagement ring and a marriage proposal. "He came up here like Sir Galahad, but who asked him to rescue me?" wrote Dian. Instead of marrying him, she sent Alexie packing— and strengthened her resolve to stay with the gorillas.

A female mountain gorilla feeds in the wilds of her Virunga Mountain habitat.

Home Sweet Home

In spring of 1968, Dian's friend Alyette de Munck paid for a permanent building at Karisoke. To Dian, this 12-by-20-foot (3.7-by-6-m) cabin was a castle compared to the tents she'd called home for the past two years.

* Roughly translated from the Kinyarwanda language, "Nyiramachabelli" means "The woman who lives alone on the mountain."

Dian's Dear Friends

After they met in 1967, Dian Fossey and Alyette de Munck became lifelong friends.

Born in Belgium, Alyette had spent most of her life in Africa, first in Congo, later in Rwanda. She met Dian shortly after her husband died. In the aftermath of his death and, several months later, the brutal killing of her son by Congolese soldiers, she threw herself into helping Dian set up her camp at Karisoke.

Over the years, Alyette, a self-taught naturalist and photographer, often visited Dian at Karisoke. The two women ate and drank together, chatted and laughed. Alyette also brought Dian supplies, served as her interpreter on occasion, and accompanied her to observe gorillas.

Alyette knew Africa, its people, politics, and traditions better than Dian did. She knew that locals needed to farm and hunt to survive. She often tried—in vain—to talk Dian into relaxing her war on poachers.

Another friend, Rosamond Carr, whom Dian also met in 1967, agreed with Alyette. She, too, had spent most of her life in Africa. Like Alyette, she cautioned Dian about interfering with the lifestyle of the local people. Despite their differences, Dian remained close friends with Rosamond and Alyette for the rest of her life.

Field Notes

Dian labeled her habituated gorilla groups (those that had become used to her) Group 4, Group 5, Group 8, and Group 9. There were also groups numbered 6 and 10. They mostly stayed away from the research area, however, and Dian spent little time observing them. Group 7 didn't exist. It turned out that the gorillas Dian had assigned to Group 7 were a few wandering members of Group 5 that she hadn't recognized.

Every day, Dian set out from her cabin to track and observe gorillas. By the end of the summer, she had identified four gorilla family groups and habituated them, which meant that the gorillas became used to Dian's presence. Using the same techniques she had used at Kabara—mimicking the animals' movements, eating habits, and grooming behavior—Dian was able to get close enough to these groups to observe them.

A view of Dian's research camp at Karisoke, on the Rwanda side of the Virunga Mountains. It would be her home in Africa for the rest of her life.

By getting closer to gorillas than anyone had in the past, Dian made many new discoveries about the animals and their behavior. She discovered, for example, that gorillas love to play—with each other, and with anything unusual they find. She had to be careful what she set down, because one of the gorillas might grab it! One day, Dian wrote, one of them "tried to pull my boot from the tree, which proved frustrating as I was wearing it."

Her work was so groundbreaking that, in September 1968, *National Geographic* magazine sent a photographer named Bob Campbell to do a photo shoot of Dian and the gorillas. Bob had been born in Scotland but now made his home in Nairobi, Kenya, with his wife. He arrived at

Another view of Dian's Karisoke camp. She is shown with her dog, Cindy, probably sometime in the late 1970s.

DIAN'S DAD

After her parents' divorce when she was six, Dian never saw her father George. One day in 1959, when she was 27, she got a letter from him out of the blue. He had spent more than 18 months tracking her down in Louisville.

George told Dian that he now lived in Inverness, just north of San Francisco, and that he had remarried "to a very wonderful person, and we are very happy." He hoped to see Dian one day. He wanted to get to know her now that he had found her. He begged her to write to him.

After that, Dian and her father wrote letters back and forth. She had a soft spot for him and always kept a photograph of him by her side.

In the summer of 1968, while she was living at Karisoke, she got a telegram from her stepmother. It said that George had killed himself. Even though she barely knew her father, Dian was devastated.

Karisoke just as Dian was leaving for a two-month break.

Bob agreed to house-sit at Dian's camp while she traveled to the United States to visit her parents—and a dentist. That way, Dian had a trustworthy person at the research camp, and Bob could spend lots of time photographing the gorillas.

During her time in America, it was clear that Dian was a changed woman. At first, she stopped in Louisville, where she had lived for 11 years. She felt uncomfortable there, even with her friends in the Henry family. They didn't share her enthusiasm for the gorillas, and by now, that was all Dian cared about.

Next, Dian traveled to California to visit her mother and stepfather. She fought with them the whole time she was there. She felt that they did not understand or appreciate her work. In reality, her parents were terrified for their 36-year-old daughter's safety. They begged her to leave Africa, and they scolded her for rejecting Alexie's marriage proposal.

Throughout her trip to the United States, Dian was annoyed with almost everyone she met. She had no patience with people who only cared about themselves and their own lives. "When I get back to civilization, I'm always appalled by 'me, me, me,'" she told an interviewer.

Dian's preference for animals over people was confirmed during this trip. She couldn't wait to get back to her beloved gorillas.

The day after she returned to Karisoke, in November 1968, Bob Campbell went home to Nairobi. In the coming months, though, he and Dian kept in touch, writing letters back and forth. Dian wrote to Bob with updates about the gorillas' activities, along with rants about the tourists who were constantly arriving, disturbing her work, and demanding she take them to see gorillas. She also wrote to Bob about her frustration with poachers.

A year earlier, when she had first set up her camp at Karisoke, Dian quickly learned that she wasn't the only human in the area. The mountain was in a protected national park. It was supposed to be a safe refuge for the gorillas, but farmers drove their cattle up the slopes to graze, destroying gorilla habitat. Hunters also set snares and traps in the area to catch other

A young girl in a poachers' camp is shown holding a severed gorilla foot. Gorillas were often killed so that their body parts could be sold to tourists as trophies. Scenes like this were much more common during the time when Dian began aggressively fighting poaching in lands that were supposed to be safe, protected habitats for gorillas.

animals, often hurting or killing gorillas in the process.

Worst of all, though, were the poachers. They deliberately killed adult gorillas so they could steal their babies for zoos in other countries. Poachers also sold gorillas' body parts to tourists who wanted exotic trophies, and to locals for use in potions, talismans, and dark rituals.

Dian despised poachers before she'd even arrived at Karisoke. She had dealt with them and their deadly ways during her short time at Kabara. Now, her rage against them grew. She began to focus more and more of her attention on doing whatever she had to do to protect the gorillas from them.

Coco and Pucker Puss

Early in 1969, Dian's hatred for poachers reached a peak. On February 24, she received a message from a friend in a nearby town. He told her that a desperately ill baby gorilla was being held in a park warden's office. The baby needed Dian's help.

The next day, Dian made her way to the park office. There, she found an infant male gorilla so sick he would not last more than a few more days without proper care. German tourists had hired poachers to provide a gorilla for a zoo in the city of Cologne. The poachers had slaughtered this little gorilla's parents and family when they tried to protect him from being captured.

The poachers had bound the baby's hands and feet. He had been kept in a cage so small that he couldn't move. His wounds were infected. He was terrified, starving, and dehydrated.

Outraged at the state of the little gorilla, Dian convinced the park official to let her take the baby and nurse him back to health.

She converted a storeroom in her cabin into a nursery and put her fieldwork on hold. If the baby was to survive, he needed all of Dian's attention. She named her new charge Coco.

This baby gorilla, like Coco, was orphaned when poachers killed his mother and hid him in an oil drum at their camp. There he was rescued by patrollers looking for gorillas that had been caught or harmed by poachers. The baby was so young that he still depended on his mother to feed him. Sadly, without enough time to become properly weaned, or accustomed to food other than his mother's milk, the baby died soon after this photo was taken.

A few days later, a group of poachers arrived with *another* baby gorilla they'd captured for the Cologne zoo. This one, a two-year-old female, was in better shape than Coco, but like Coco, she was wounded where her hands and feet had been bound. She had also been slashed with a machete, which is a large knife. Dian named this second little gorilla Pucker Puss, or Pucker for short.

For the next two months, Dian looked after Coco and Pucker, feeding them, giving them medicine, and caring for their every need. In effect, "I play mother gorilla," she wrote to Louis Leakey.

Caring for Coco and Pucker was a full-time job. While they were with her, Dian had no time to observe the gorilla family groups in the wild. "But I'm filling up notebooks on the behavior of these two monsters, which of course is almost identical to that of wild infants and fascinating to observe at such close quarters!"

In fact, what Dian learned from her interactions with Coco and Pucker significantly advanced her knowledge of gorilla behavior.

As the youngsters began to recover, Dian started writing officials at the Cologne zoo. She begged them to let her keep the young gorillas and return them to the wild one day. Her pleas fell on deaf ears. Early in May, the local park warden forced her to hand over Coco and Pucker. The babies were put on a plane and sent to live in a German zoo.

Dian was shattered by this turn of events, and her hatred of poachers increased.

(Coco and Pucker died at the zoo nine years later, within a month of each other—well short of their 30-year life expectancy.)

By the time the two young gorillas were shipped out to Germany, photographer Bob Campbell had returned to Karisoke to continue his work for *National Geographic.* At the time, he and Dian did not enjoy each other's company. At the end of April, she wrote to her parents: "Honestly, he is the biggest bore I've ever met and his dull, old-lady ways really have had me going around the bend.... I don't think two more incompatible [poorly suited or matched] people could have been thrown together."

A month later, Bob wrote about Dian to a colleague at the National Geographic Society: "She can be abrupt and rude, then a few hours later, as sweet as you like…. I guess I'll have to grin and bear it."

He went on to call her "the most unusual and mixed up person I have come across in years." Later in his letter, though, he admitted to having some admiration for Dian, given the

This close-up of a gorilla's hand clutching a vine offers a powerful reminder of how many characteristics of these remarkable animals are similar to those of humans.

PEANUTS

In the first week of January 1970, Dian experienced one of the most memorable moments of her life. One day, as she and Bob Campbell were tracking gorillas, a male named Peanuts approached Dian and started making a fuss. "He beat his chest and threw leaves in the air, he swaggered and slapped the foliage around him," wrote Dian. "Suddenly he was at my side." To entertain him, Dian made noises and scratched herself.

"Then, I lay back in the foliage to appear as harmless as possible and slowly extended my hand." She looked away and made no sounds or movements. "Finally, he came a step closer and … gently touched his fingers to mine." This was the first known instance of a gorilla and human touching or "holding hands."

Dian was so thrilled and moved by the experience that she burst into happy tears. The best part was that Bob had caught the entire interaction on camera. The photo of Dian and Peanuts touching hands is one of the most famous photographs of Bob's career.

Dian is shown photographing and relaxing with a group of mountain gorillas at their Virunga habitat in Rwanda. Photos like this—as well as the images she took herself—helped Dian draw attention to her campaign to protect gorillas from poachers. They also, however, fueled people's curiosity about the gorillas, which further intruded on their habitat.

difficulties of her work and the conditions at Karisoke: "I can think of very few people who would have had the guts to carry on as she has done."

For the rest of 1969, Bob spent a great deal of time at Karisoke, continuing his photography project. Over the months, he and Dian gradually got used to each other and even began to enjoy each other's company. Before the year was out, the two became involved romantically, despite the fact that, as Bob put it, "I was happily married and loved my wife."

Fame and Pain

In January 1970, *National Geographic* ran a story Dian had written about the mountain gorillas. A collection of Bob's photos ran alongside her article. On the cover of the magazine was a photo of Dian with Coco and Pucker. She was thrilled that the publication had chosen to highlight this tender photo of her and the babies.

Because of this magazine feature—and others that were to follow—Dian, her work, and the gorillas became international celebrities. Whenever she left Karisoke, she was in demand as a guest speaker, and students around the globe clamored for the chance to work with her in the Virunga Mountains of Rwanda.

Dian tolerated the publicity because of the attention it drew to the need to help the gorillas—and the money it brought in. She barely tolerated the students, and only because she needed help with her gorilla observations and with her fight against poachers.

> *"The gorilla is one of the most maligned animals in the world. After more than 2,000 hours of direct observation, I can account for less than five minutes of what might be called 'aggressive' behavior.... Naturally an animal is going to try to protect itself, and there are a number of recorded instances of gorillas attacking humans when the latter hunted them. And there are the tales of the 'intrepid white hunters' who have 'courageously' faced the screaming charges of the white-fanged hairy ape-man. The result is the common, and quite false, picture of the introverted, peaceful vegetarian that I have come to know."*
>
> Dian Fossey, *National Geographic*, January 1970

Just before the *National Geographic* article appeared, Dian left Karisoke to begin a graduate degree at Cambridge University in England. For the next several years, she split her time between Cambridge and Karisoke.

At first, Bob looked after the research camp when Dian was away—and he often stayed with her there upon her return. Before long, he and Dian fell in love. She wanted Bob to leave his wife, something he had no intention of doing.

Instead, in the spring of 1972, Bob left Karisoke, never to return. "Never have I known such sorrow," Dian wrote at the time.

Instantly, her mood and attitude changed. She began drinking heavily and rarely left her cabin. She refused to see anyone and left the gorilla observations to her staff and students.

After two months of this behavior, Dian finally emerged from her cabin and got back to work. Still, for the next few years, her actions—and her health—spiraled downward.

She angered easily, lost interest in the gorillas, and became abusive toward her students and staff. She continued to drink and smoke heavily. She suffered stress fractures in her legs from all the hard work and mountain climbing she did. She contracted emphysema, a smoking-related lung disease, and often fell ill with other conditions. She also had another short-lived love affair with another married man.

At the same time, Dian stepped up her fight against poachers. She also stepped up her fight against the farmers whose cattle wandered through mountain gorilla habitat. At first, she merely chased the cows away. Then she started spray-painting them to discourage the herders from bringing them into the protected park.

FIELD NOTES

In early 1971, Louis Leakey was to visit Dian during one of her stays at Cambridge. Instead, Dian ended up visiting him in a hospital in London after he suffered a heart attack at the airport. He recovered quickly and returned to work. In October 1972, Louis had another heart attack. This time, sadly, he died.

THE EDUCATION OF DIAN

Even though Dian had devoted much of her life to the study of mountain gorillas, she had no formal scientific qualifications. She and Louis Leakey felt that, for her to be taken seriously within the scientific community, she needed a graduate degree. "Without a Ph.D., it is very hard to get adequate grant support or to get really good students to come and work on your project," Dian said.

In January 1970, she began a Ph.D., or doctorate, program at Cambridge University in the UK. Her graduate supervisor, Robert Hinde, had also been Jane Goodall's supervisor.

Dian graduated from Cambridge with a Ph.D. in zoology with her study of mountain gorilla behavior. There is some dispute about the year in which she actually received her degree. Some sources give the year as 1974. Others report that she defended her dissertation in 1976. This means that she passed the final oral exam based on the long research work she wrote to complete her doctoral studies.

Later, she began shooting over the heads of the cows, hoping to scare the animals away. At one point, Dian resorted to shooting cows dead—but this was so far against her animal-loving nature that she vowed never to do it again.

She had less sympathy for the poachers.

Active Conservation

Since she had first arrived at Karisoke, Dian and her helpers had tirelessly cut every snare and trap they found. Dian also complained about poachers to park staff, who were often in on the poaching and did nothing to halt it.

When this didn't stop the poachers, Dian launched an aggressive anti-poaching crusade that became more and more violent. She and her staff continued to cut traps and snares, but Dian started terrorizing the people who set them. She chased the poachers, shot at them, and hired anti-poaching patrols to help her. She called this hard-line approach "active conservation."

Dian and members of her anti-poaching patrol are shown with some of the snares they have cut and seized. Dian called her increasingly aggressive approach to fighting poachers "active conservation."

> *"Active conservation [of gorillas] involves simply going out into the forest, on foot, day after day after day, attempting to capture poachers, killing—regretfully—poacher dogs, which spread rabies within the park, and cutting down traps."*
>
> Dian Fossey

At one point she set fire to one man's possessions and kidnapped his four-year-old son. She kept the boy for one night before sending him home. She later referred to this incident as her "worst no-no."

Dian also played on the fears and superstitions of the local people in her efforts to protect the gorillas. The people in the area believed in magic and feared anyone they thought had magical powers. To take advantage of those fears, Dian bought Halloween masks, magic tricks, firecrackers, and noisemakers whenever she visited the United States and Cambridge. She used these trinkets to terrify the locals, many of whom believed Dian was a witch. She hoped they would fear her "powers" enough to do as she wished and stop poaching and hunting.

That didn't happen. The reality was that the local people had to feed their families. Cattle farming and poaching were among the only ways they had to make a living. To preserve their livelihood, they began to strike back against Dian's anti-poaching tactics. She endured thefts from her camp, vandalism, dognapping, and revenge killings of her beloved gorillas.

On December 31, 1977, though, the poachers went too far.

Digit

Over the years, mountain gorilla Group 4 became Dian's favorite—to the point that she considered this group of animals to be her family. In the late 1970s, as her spirit declined and her health deteriorated, she focused even more on Group 4, leaving students and staff to observe the others. Dian was particularly close to one member of this group, a young gorilla named Digit.

Dian had first met Digit in 1967. At the time, he was a charming little five-year-old. Dian named him Digit because he had a damaged finger on his right hand. As the years passed, Digit became Dian's best gorilla friend. He was a funny little ape, playful, curious, and cheeky. He would often touch Dian's clothing or hair, or hug her. He liked her to play with him and tickle him.

In 1972, before Bob Campbell departed from Karisoke for the last time, he took a number of photos of Digit. Two years later, the government of Rwanda began using those photos on posters to promote tourism. The posters featured a picture of Digit with the words, "Come and Meet Him in Rwanda."

As Digit grew up, he became a leader within his family group, taking responsibility for the females and young gorillas. He began to draw

Justice for Digit

In the days following Digit's murder, Dian and her staff captured a poacher. Under intense questioning, he admitted that he and five others had killed Digit. They killed him because a local merchant wanted a silverback gorilla's head and hands to sell to tourists. He paid the poachers the equivalent of $20 for the body parts. Four of the six poachers went to jail for Digit's murder.

Dian buried Digit's body in a graveyard (shown here) beside her cabin.

away from most humans, but he and Dian still maintained their relationship.

On New Year's Day, 1978, Dian stayed at camp, awaiting the arrival of a television film crew. Meanwhile, one of her trackers and a student named Ian Redmond went in search of Group 4. Instead, they found a bloody trail— and the butchered body of Digit.

The 15-year-old gorilla's head, hands, and feet had been chopped off. His body was pierced with spear wounds. He had died protecting his family from poachers. The other 13 members of Group 4 survived the attack.

Dian was grief-stricken when Ian told her about Digit's murder. She wrote:

> *"There are times when one cannot accept facts for fear of shattering one's being. As I listened to Ian's terrible words, all of Digit's life, since my first meeting with him as a playful little ball of black fluff ten years earlier, poured through my mind. From that dreadful moment on, I came to live within an insulated part of myself."*

From that moment on, too, she declared all-out war on poachers.

Chapter 5
Gorillas in the Mist

By the time he died, on or around New Year's Eve, 1977, Digit was almost as famous as Dian Fossey was. His photos had been featured in *National Geographic* magazine, and he was the poster boy for Rwandan tourism. A month after he was killed, Digit's murder was the headline story on the CBS evening news. This was a remarkable moment in the history of wildlife conservation. A decade earlier, few people even knew that mountain gorillas existed. Now, Digit's senseless killing captured the attention—and fury—of animal lovers around the globe.

A baby gorilla in Volcano National Park in Rwanda.

Conflict at Karisoke

Dian used the world's outrage over Digit's death to raise money for her "active conservation" of mountain gorillas. She created the Digit Fund,

Dian plays with a baby gorilla at her Karisoke research camp. The cruel and tragic killing of Digit sparked news reports and outrage around the world. It also brought attention and donations to Dian's efforts to protect mountain gorillas.

and donations from around the world poured in. Dian used the money to hire, train, outfit, and pay locals to cut traps and seize weapons from poachers. She increased foot patrols within the protected park area.

When Dian had first arrived in Africa 12 years earlier, she had poured her passion into studying mountain gorillas in the wild. Now, the identification and punishment of poachers became her obsession, her reason for living.

She insisted that every poacher the patrols found be brought to her for questioning. Rumors began to circulate that she was torturing and beating the guilty hunters, not just interviewing them.

In July 1978, almost seven months after Digit's death, Dian's staff found two more Group 4 gorillas murdered. The group's leader, a silverback named Uncle Bert, and his mate Macho had been shot.

Uncle Bert's head had also been cut off. Bert and Macho's baby, Kweli, was wounded in the attack. He died from infection three months later.

All three were buried with Digit in the graveyard next to Dian's cabin.

FIELD NOTES

Digit's mate Simba gave birth to Digit's baby in the spring of 1978. Dian named the baby Mwelu, which means "a touch of brightness and light."

The reasons for this set of murders weren't clear. Many people assumed the trio was killed in revenge for Dian's war on poachers. Others thought the poachers hoped the dead gorillas would somehow earn them money. Dian believed the poachers were after baby Kweli, but abandoned him when he was wounded.

Regardless of the reason, these deaths, along with Digit's killing, spelled the end of Dian's beloved Group 4. By the end of the year, the remaining gorillas in this family had joined other groups. Without Uncle Bert and Digit to guide and protect them, the female gorillas and their young needed to find new homes and new mates.

As Dian stepped up her active conservation methods, others at Karisoke took a different approach to protecting mountain gorillas.

In late January 1978, a new pair of students arrived—Americans Bill Weber and Amy Vedder. Bill's goal was to start a census, or count, of the remaining mountain gorillas. Amy wanted to observe and study Group 5.

The couple also wanted to set up a gorilla tourism program. By this time, the Rwandan government allowed tourists to visit Group 5, but there were no proper procedures in place.

Left: Dian prepares a grave marker for one of her gorillas. Right: Over the years, the graveyard at Dian's camp grew to include many more gorillas. Many, sadly, died years short of their natural lifespan, some just a few years after being born.

Tourists wandered about as they pleased, disturbing the researchers and the animals.

Bill and Amy wanted to create a *controlled* gorilla tourism program—with time limits on visits, restrictions on where tourists could go, and caps on the number of visitors allowed into the park at any one time. They also planned to launch an education program for locals, to prove to them that the gorillas had more value alive than dead.

They reasoned that, if tourists would pay to see gorillas, locals would start protecting them, and poachers would stop killing them. The couple believed this plan would have a longer-term effect on the gorillas' survival than Dian's more violent approach.

Others at Karisoke, and within the Rwandan government, agreed with Bill and Amy.

Dian didn't see it this way. She saw tourists as invaders. They bothered the gorillas and brought human diseases that the gorillas couldn't fight.

She made it clear that she intended the focus of gorilla protection to continue to be on stopping poachers, using whatever tactics necessary. After the violent deaths of Uncle Bert and Macho, capturing and punishing poachers became her only concern.

These clashing approaches to protecting gorillas caused much conflict at Karisoke. Over the months, tensions rose to the point that Dian barely spoke to Bill and Amy.

At the same time her health was in rapid decline. She had trouble breathing because of her smoking. She had broken bones that hadn't healed properly and were causing her pain.

Good for Humans, Not So Good for Gorillas

Throughout her career, Dian Fossey opposed gorilla tourism—allowing paying visitors to observe the great apes at close quarters. She feared that humans would bring disease to the animals.

Because gorillas are so closely related to humans, they have been known to catch human illnesses, such as colds, flu, stomach ailments, skin diseases, and tuberculosis.

Because gorillas have no immunity to these diseases, they can die from them. At least two mountain gorillas have died after catching respiratory illnesses from humans. Tourists in Virunga National Park are now required to wear surgical face masks when visiting gorillas.

Parasites transmitted to gorillas through the bodily waste of careless humans have also killed gorillas.

Not only do humans pose physical dangers to these animals, but they also inflict emotional harm. A 2010 study concluded that "Gorillas are being dangerously stressed by tourists whose attentions are disrupting the animals' feeding routines and making them aggressive." The researchers suggested increasing the minimum distance between humans and gorillas from 23 feet (7 m) to 59 feet (18 m). This has not happened.

Accompanied by their guide, tourists are shown photographing mountain gorillas in Virunga National Park, Rwanda. This photo was taken before tourists were required to wear surgical face masks in the presence of gorillas. It illustrates the concern of Dian and other animal rights activists over the invasion of humans into the natural habitats of mountain gorillas.

COMPETITION FOR GORILLA DOLLARS

Around the time Dian Fossey founded the Digit Fund, one of her former students founded the Mountain Gorilla Preservation Fund (MGPF). Its goal was to raise money to help gorillas, although it didn't have a clear plan for doing so. What it did have was the support of Britain's most successful conservation group, the Fauna and Flora Preservation Society. Because of this, the MGPF raised a lot of money very quickly—but it competed with the Digit Fund for contributions.

The MGPF gave much of its money to the Rwandan government's parks department, and to another new organization— the Mountain Gorilla Project, founded by Bill Weber and Amy Vedder in 1979. Its mission was to educate locals about the value of living gorillas, and to attract tourists to Rwanda to see them.

In 1980, the leader of yet another organization, the African Wildlife Leadership Foundation, suggested that Dian merge the Digit Fund with his foundation. She refused this offer.

Today, the Digit Fund continues to fight for funds with a number of other groups, including the International Gorilla Conservation Programme. This organization was created in 1991 when the MGPF, the Fauna and Flora group, and the Mountain Gorilla Project—along with the World Wildlife Fund— joined together to create a united gorilla conservation organization.

She had a kidney infection. She was weak and tired.

By the end of 1978, Dian's body was such a wreck that she rarely went into the field to observe gorillas any more.

Homeward Bound

As Dian's physical health declined, her mental health also came into question. Bill and Amy, for example, expressed concern over "the deeply disturbed mental state of Dian Fossey." Comments like this may have been merely an attempt to hurt Dian's reputation—and that is exactly what began to happen. Reports of Dian's increasingly violent and erratic behavior started to emerge. Her family, friends, and coworkers began to question her sanity.

> *"The man who kills the animals today is the man who kills the people who get in his way tomorrow."*
>
> Dian Fossey

Meanwhile, Dian's anti-poaching campaign was becoming an embarrassment to the organizations that supported her. In the spring of 1979, the Leakey Foundation and the National Geographic Society threatened to cut her funding.

At the same time, the scientific community was pressuring Dian to write up the results of her years of research, and an editor was insisting she finish writing a book she had started.

Knowing she needed a break, all these people pressed Dian to leave Africa. Her problem was that she didn't know where to go when she left Karisoke.

In August of that year, a professor from Cornell University in Ithaca, New York, visited Karisoke. He solved Dian's problem by offering her a job as a visiting professor at Cornell.

Dian accepted the offer, and in March 1980, to everyone's relief, she packed up and moved to Ithaca. There, Dian taught classes and interacted with spellbound students while catching up on her writing in her free time. She settled into her life there—as much as she could without her gorilla friends.

> *"For people who come to my lectures, a gorilla isn't just a stack of scientific data. It is alive. They can feel for it in life and death. They care about Digit and Uncle Bert and all the rest. My book can help them do the same."*
>
> Dian Fossey, while in
> Ithaca, New York

In July, Dian made a quick visit to Karisoke, only to discover that her pet monkey Kima had died, and her dog Cindy was sick. Devastated by yet another loss in her life, Dian refused to leave Cindy behind again. When she returned to New York a few days later, she took the elderly pooch with her.

In the summer of 1981, Dian finally finished writing a book about her work with the mountain gorillas. *Gorillas in the Mist* was published two years later and became an international bestseller.

While Dian enjoyed her time in Ithaca—and was healthier than she had been in years—she knew she didn't belong there. After Cindy died in October 1982, she felt there was no reason for her to stay in the United States. Her heart was

Dian stands outside her cabin at Karisoke with her beloved dog, Cindy. In 1980, after Dian had accepted a position at Cornell University, she returned briefly to Karisoke, learned that Cindy was ill, and took her canine companion with her when she returned to the United States.

FIELD NOTES

Dian Fossey didn't just hang out with mountain gorillas while she was in Africa. During her years at Karisoke, she kept a number of pets—a dog named Cindy; a monkey named Kima; a pair of ravens, Charles and Yvonne; and two gray parrots called Dot and Dash. She also had a pair of chickens, named Lucy and Dezi, who were supposed to be dinner, but Dian couldn't bring herself to eat them.

WOMAN OF THE RED APE

Birute Galdikas was born in Germany in 1946 and raised in Canada. She attended the University of California, Los Angeles. When she was a graduate student in anthropology at UCLA, Birute met Louis Leakey. She convinced him to launch a study of orangutans in Borneo—with her as the researcher.

In 1971, Birute and her photographer husband landed in the jungles of Borneo to begin field studies of the red ape, or orangutan. With that, Birute became the third of Louis's so-called trimates—the three women he commissioned (including Jane Goodall and Dian Fossey) to study great apes in their natural habitats.

Little was known about the orangutans before Birute began her studies. She learned that the animals spend about half of each day on the ground, the other half in trees. At night, they sleep in nests in branches high above the jungle floor. Orangutans eat fruit, flowers, bark, leaves, and insects. They can live 30 to 50 years, and the males can stand five feet (1.5 m) tall. Females bear a single baby every eight or nine years.

Birute has lived at her research site in Borneo for more than 40 years, although she now spends about half her time in North America. She remains a passionate champion of the orangutans and the preservation of their habitat.

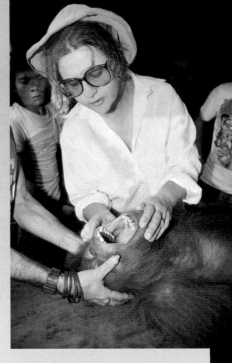

Birute Galdikas gives a young adult orangutan a dental exam at Camp Leakey, the research and rehabilitation center she established in the 1970s on the part of the island of Borneo that is in Indonesia.

Orangutans at Camp Leakey.

SILENCE PLEASE ! RESPECT THE ORANGUTANS !

TRIMATES TOGETHER

During the 1970s and 1980s, scientific organizations brought Louis Leakey's so-called "trimates" together on three separate occasions. The trimates were the three women Louis had commissioned to conduct long-term studies of the world's great apes: Jane Goodall, who studied chimpanzees; Dian Fossey, who studied mountain gorillas; and Birute Galdikas, who studied orangutans.

Whenever the three women came together, they drew crowds.

Their first joint symposium took place in California in May 1976. At the second, in Virginia in April 1981, the women's topic was "What We Can Learn About Humankind from the Apes." At their final collective presentation, in New York City in May 1982, they talked about the daily lives and special characteristics of each of the great apes, focusing on the ways that the animals resembled humans.

still with her beloved mountain gorillas in Rwanda. She knew it was time to return to them.

In June 1983, just before *Gorillas in the Mist* hit bookstores, she made a short visit to Karisoke. "The return was very emotional as I once again met my African staff, some of whom have worked for the camp since 1967," she wrote. "We simultaneously hugged one another, shook hands, cried, laughed, and exchanged all kinds of gossip and tales."

After the joyful reunion, along with a meal and time to freshen up, Dian took a good look around Karisoke. As happy as she was to reunite with her longtime colleagues, "my heart really sank" at the state of the research camp. "I have never imagined such decay and neglect," she wrote. "The whole camp has been totally neglected as white people have come and gone, taken what they wanted, never bothering to replace or refurbish [restore] anything."

During Dian's time in Ithaca, Karisoke had seen several acting camp directors come and go. Dian did not like most of them, nor did she approve of their methods. They had different priorities than she did. They spent what little money they had on increasing tourism and education, rather than on gorilla protection and maintaining the research station. "Everything I worked for nearly single-handedly over thirteen years is just about finished," said Dian, who immediately began cleaning up the camp.

A month later, Dian set out to visit the gorillas of Group 5 for the first time since her return. "Would they remember me after three years' absence?" she wondered. "I doubted it sincerely."

Within minutes, though, her fears were eased. Two of the older females dropped everything as soon as they saw her. They walked toward Dian, stared into her eyes,

"Whenever I am away, people try to take over Karisoke—nine cabins and 12 perfectly trained Africans. I need to re-establish my 'clout' [power] here with Europeans who want to take over the camp, the gorillas, and the trained Africans."

Dian Fossey, February 1984, in a letter to her parents, explaining why she must stay at Karisoke

and hugged her! "I could have happily died right then and there and wished for nothing more on earth, simply because they had remembered," she wrote. "I know now that I've truly come home."

She decided then and there that Karisoke was where she belonged—and where she would spend the rest of her life.

Chapter 6
No One Loved Gorillas More

After Dian's book, *Gorillas in the Mist*, was released in August 1983, her publisher sent her on a whirlwind speaking tour. For six months, Dian blazed through the United States, the UK, and South Africa. It was hectic and exhausting—and all she wanted to do was get back to her gorillas. Finally, in February 1984, the book tour ended, and Dian returned to Karisoke.

Dian poses in front of a large stuffed gorilla at the American Museum of Natural History in New York City in early 1984. At this time, she was near the end of her speaking tour to promote Gorillas in the Mist *and would soon be heading back to her camp at Karisoke.*

"Dian kufa! Dian kufa!"

Everyone who worked with Dian in Rwanda hoped that her stay in the United States had softened her personality and her methods of protecting the gorillas. It had not.

When she returned to Karisoke, Dian renewed her opposition to gorilla tourism and continued to clash with park officials, government administrators, researchers, and even tourists. The Rwandan government granted her permission to stay in Rwanda for shorter and shorter periods of time. Even the National Geographic Society and the Leakey Foundation were no longer on Dian's side. In spring 1984, a few months after she returned to Karisoke, they cut off her funding.

Dian continued to finance her war on poachers using money she earned from her book sales, the Digit Fund, and an inheritance from her *real* Uncle Bert, for whom the gorilla had been named.

Many people believed it was time for Dian to turn Karisoke over to younger researchers once and for all. Of course, she had no intention of doing so. Karisoke was Dian's home. Still, she took a few short trips away from the research camp over the next two years.

In 1984, she visited the United States twice—to seek funding, visit her parents, consult with a doctor about her health, and accept an award from the Humane Society of the United States. This was the first such honor Dian had ever received. Six months later, the Humane Society of New York awarded her a special gold medal in honor of her conservation work with mountain gorillas.

In the summer of 1985, Dian made another visit to the United States—an all-expense paid trip to California to speak at a fundraising dinner. She appeared on *The Tonight Show* while she was there, visited her parents, and had surgery on one of her eyes. This would be her last time away from Karisoke.

In September of that year, 53-year-old Dian visited her gorillas for the last time. Her health had declined to the point that she could no longer climb into the mountains without an oxygen tank to help her breathe. She was thin and frail and could barely walk because of leg and joint pain.

Still, come December, she managed to prepare for her annual Karisoke Christmas party. Up to 100 guests attended her yearly holiday celebration, which always included decorations, carols sung in many languages, a feast with banana beer, and gifts for everyone.

This year, the party was to be held on New Year's Day instead of Christmas Day. A

FIELD NOTES

Within a year of the 1983 publication of *Gorillas in the Mist*, the book had been translated into six languages. By 1984, a film version was in the works, with Sigourney Weaver playing Dian. Released in 1988, the movie won two Golden Globe awards and was nominated for five Oscars. Its theatrical release poster is shown here.

SIGOURNEY WEAVER · BRYAN BROWN

In a land of beauty, wonder and danger, she would follow a dream, fall in love and risk her life to save the mountain gorillas from extinction.

The true adventure of Dian Fossey.

GORILLAS IN THE MIST

film crew was arriving on January 1, and Dian wanted the group to be included in the festivities.

On Christmas Day, she had a quiet dinner with her two graduate students. One was a Rwandan who had been with her since July, the other an American named Wayne McGuire, who had arrived at Karisoke a month later.

The two young men spent the following day in the field counting gorillas, while Dian stayed at camp. Wayne stopped in to give Dian a report before he headed to bed that night.

The next morning, December 27, 1985, just after six o'clock, Wayne woke to the sound of screams. "Dian kufa! Dian kufa!" *Dian is dead*!

He ran to her cabin, where he discovered Dian lying on the floor, a gun by her side and a long gash through her skull.

> *"When you realize the value of all life, you dwell less on what is past and concentrate on the preservation of the future."*
>
> Dian's final journal entry before her death

An Unsolved Mystery

Dian was murdered with her own machete, a broad blade she had seized from a poacher years earlier. The killer had hit her over the head several times, almost splitting her skull in two. It appeared that Dian had tried to load her gun to defend herself but hadn't had time.

The wall of her cabin had been sliced open for the killer to gain entry—in one of the few places where no furniture stood against the wall to block the way. The cabin was tossed about, but nothing was taken. Because of these factors, officials believed Dian was killed by someone who knew her, the cabin's layout, and the camp's routine.

DIAN AND DIGIT, SIDE-BY-SIDE

Dian Fossey's funeral and burial took place on December 31, 1985—eight years to the day after Digit was killed. Dian was buried in a grave beside her best gorilla friend, in the cemetery next to her cabin at Karisoke. A number of friends, staff, students, and former researchers attended her funeral.

Memorial services were also held for Dian in New York, Washington, D.C., and California.

Dian's gravestone reads as follows:

"'Nyiramachabelli.' No one loved gorillas more. Rest in peace dear friend, eternally protected in this sacred ground, for you are home where you belong."

Friends and coworkers lower the coffin of Dian Fossey into the graveyard in which she had buried so many of her gorilla companions.

Dian's burial spot and marker lie within an arm's reach of the resting place of her beloved Digit.

In the following months, police interviewed every person who lived and worked at Karisoke at the time of Dian's death. In August, two were charged—one of her longtime African trackers, who was later found dead in his jail cell, and graduate student Wayne McGuire.

Early in the summer of 1986, Wayne had been tipped off that he was going to be arrested. He had fled to the United States at the end of June. In December, he was tried *in absentia*, meaning he wasn't there for the trial. He was found guilty of Dian's murder and sentenced to be shot by a firing squad if he ever returned to Rwanda. Because the United States had no extradition agreement with the African nation, Wayne was not sent back to face punishment.

Wayne has always maintained his innocence. He says he was set up because the Rwandan government did not want an African to be guilty of the terrible crime.

To this day, nobody knows for sure who killed Dian or why.

Did Wayne kill her? Or was it one of her African staff members? Many people believe a poacher murdered her in retaliation for her anti-poaching methods.

In 2001, a new theory emerged. That year, a powerful Rwandan politician and businessman named Protais Zigiranyirazo, or "Monsieur Zed" (abbreviated as "M. Z" and French for "Mr. Z"), was arrested for his part in the 1994 Rwandan Genocide. At the same time, the FBI accused him of ordering Dian's murder. In the months before her death, Dian had gathered information suggesting that M. Z was involved in the illegal trade of gold, ivory, and mountain gorillas. She had threatened to expose him. The FBI believed M. Zed had her killed for that reason, but he was never formally charged with the crime. Eventually, M. Zed was also cleared of all charges of genocide.

CRISIS IN RWANDA

In Rwanda in 1994, after years of hatred between two ethnic groups, the Hutus and the Tutsis, one of the groups set out to completely eliminate the other. In April, Hutus massacred about 800,000 Tutsis. Also killed were about 200,000 Hutus who opposed the killings. This massacre is now known as the Rwandan Genocide. It ended when a small group of Tutsi rebels managed to overthrow the Hutu leaders and take charge of the country. What makes this event even more tragic is that the rest of the world knew the genocide was happening but largely failed to intervene or do anything about it.

Photographs of victims of the Rwandan Genocide on display as part of an exhibit at the Genocide Memorial Center in Kigali, Rwanda.

Karisoke and Beyond

In the first few years following Dian's death, mountain gorilla studies continued at Karisoke. New researchers expanded on Dian's understanding of the animals' behavior, while park rangers continued to protect the gorillas from poachers. At the same time, new education programs introduced local schoolchildren to the importance of protecting the environment and the gorillas.

In 1992, the rising civil unrest in Rwanda reached Karisoke. Rebels stormed the research camp, ransacking and stealing. Researchers refused to leave. They stayed at Karisoke to continue their work with the gorillas.

Two years later, though, during the Rwandan Genocide, all staff members were forced to flee to safety. Still, some vowed to continue their research. When they returned—against all advice—they found that Karisoke had been destroyed. They rebuilt the camp, and a small, brave group continued to monitor, or keep close watch on, the gorillas.

In 1997, violence erupted across the border in Zaire (formerly Congo), once again putting a halt to research work in the area. A year later, after having fled five times and twice rebuilding Karisoke, staff and researchers finally relocated the study center to the nearby town of Ruhengeri (also called Musanze). It remains there today.

A few field study stations are still located within the Virunga Mountains gorilla habitat, but Dian's original Karisoke research camp is no more. It has been overtaken by the jungle, the buildings overgrown and in ruins. Dian's

grave is one of the few landmarks that survive on the site.

Remarkably, the mountain gorillas managed to survive the violence of the 1990s. A few were killed, but most escaped to remote, isolated parts of the jungle, too dense for humans to reach. Most have since returned to their original Virunga Mountain habitat, where thousands of tourists visit them every year. Every day, anti-poaching patrols sweep the area, while trackers check on the gorillas.

Virunga park rangers on patrol in Uganda (top) and the Democratic Republic of the Congo (bottom) to act against poachers and outlaws who illegally seize land.

FIELD NOTES

Dian Fossey's face has appeared on postage stamps in at least three countries. Palau, a set of tiny islands in the western Pacific Ocean, featured Dian in a 1999 series of stamps celebrating environmental heroes of the 20th century. In 2011, the Central African Republic included a stamp with Dian's picture in a 52-stamp "Fauna, Flora, Minerals" collection. A year later, Mozambique created a six-stamp Dian Fossey set, in honor of what would have been her 80th birthday.

PALAU
33¢

DIANE FOSSEY

Dian Fossey would be thrilled to know that the gorillas she feared would vanish by the turn of the 21st century continue to survive today. When she began her studies in 1966, only 242 gorillas existed, and the species was facing extinction. The most recent census (2010–2011) shows 480 mountain gorillas living in the Virunga Mountains, with another 400 living in a national park to the north, in Uganda. That's a total of 880 mountain gorillas. (The results of a 2015–2016 census are not yet known.)

Today, the preservation of endangered mountain gorillas is taken seriously by local people and tourism officials alike in the Virunga Mountains. In this photo, drummers of the Batwa tribe perform at a traditional dance to celebrate the birth of a mountain gorilla in November 2013 in Musanze, Rwanda. This region is where five of the eight major Virunga mountains are located, and it's home to the largest population of mountain gorillas in Rwanda.

That's not to say the mountain gorillas are not still at risk. The World Wildlife Fund labels their status as "critically endangered." The main threat to the apes is habitat loss through farming, deforestation, and illegal settlers moving into their territory. Hunting, poaching, civil war, and disease also continue to threaten the great beasts.

In addition to hunting, poaching, and other aggressive human actions, mountain gorillas are threatened by the destruction of their forest habitat. In this photo, a group of mountain gorillas is shown at the meeting point of a farm field and the forest's edge in Virunga National Park, Democratic Republic of the Congo.

POACHING PERSISTS

Despite the efforts of people like Dian Fossey, poaching continues to devastate wildlife populations in Africa. Elephants, black rhinos, lions, zebras, and gorillas are among the animals still killed for their body parts, or as trophies.

Up to 35,000 elephants are killed every year for their ivory tusks. Rhinoceros horns are also in demand. Some people believe the ingredients in rhino horns cure certain illnesses. The number of rhinos killed for their horns in 2013 was 946—that's 800 times more than the number killed a decade earlier.

Zebras are killed for their skins. Lions are killed because their habitat is being wiped out. They are hungry, so they are killing farm animals, then being shot by farmers. Adult mountain gorillas are still being killed so poachers can steal their babies.

The Convention on International Trade in Endangered Species of Wild Fauna and Flora (CITES) came into being in 1975. Today, 181 countries around the world have signed the treaty agreeing that they won't allow imports or exports of endangered species or their body parts.

This treaty has certainly slowed the buying and selling of endangered animals, but unfortunately, hasn't stopped it. As long as there are people willing to pay for animals and their body parts, poachers will continue to find ways to provide them.

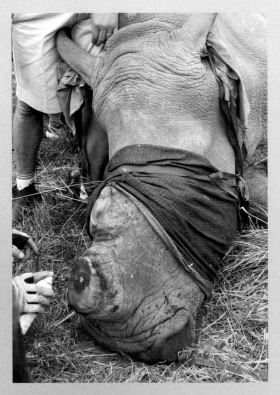

Poaching doesn't only affect animals in Africa. Wildlife around the world is targeted.

One way to stop poachers from killing rhinoceroses for their horns is for teams of vets and conservationists to remove the horn without injuring the rhino. In this photo, taken in South Africa, a rhino has had its horn painlessly removed and is receiving antiseptic spray to prevent infection.

Even though many people questioned Dian's research and conservation methods over the years, nobody questions the fact that she is one of the main reasons mountain gorillas survive today. She launched one of the world's first conservation programs, raising awareness about the dangers of habitat destruction and illegal poaching. Through the articles and books Dian wrote, the world outside Africa learned to understand—and value—these majestic beasts. Her groundbreaking study of these great apes showed that they are gentle, family-loving, and emotional beings that deserve protection.

NO PLAN B FOR MOUNTAIN GORILLAS IN ZOOS

In zoos around the world, visitors get to see gorillas. Some zoos have even successfully bred gorillas. These animals, however, are lowland gorillas, not mountain gorillas. No zoo has ever been able to keep a mountain gorilla alive in captivity for more than a few years. Scientists don't yet know the reason for this. It could be that mountain gorillas are more sensitive to disease or emotional stress. This means that unlike many other rare species, it is not possible to protect and breed these critically endangered animals in zoos. The only hope for mountain gorillas is that they be allowed to live wild lives in their natural mountain home.

Funding Gorilla Protection

In 1978, after the death of Digit, her favorite gorilla, Dian Fossey founded the Digit Fund. She used the money to support research at Karisoke and to pay for anti-poaching patrols in mountain gorilla habitat. The fund was renamed the Dian Fossey Gorilla Fund in 1992, seven years after Dian's death.

The fund continues its original work but has expanded to include health and education programs, economic development in local communities, and reforestation projects. The goal is to help gorillas and local people thrive and live healthily side-by-side.

Field Notes

On January 16, 2014, as a tribute to Dian on what would have been her 82nd birthday, Google created a Google Doodle in her honor.

"There can be no doubt whatsoever that Dian did more to save the mountain gorillas than anyone," wrote her colleague Jane Goodall. "All of us who care about these amazing beings, and their preservation in the wild, owe Dian a huge debt of gratitude."

No one loved gorillas more.

"*There would be no mountain gorillas in the Virungas today ... were it not for Dian Fossey's tireless efforts over many years.*"

Robinson McIlvaine, former president of the African Wildlife Foundation

Chronology

January 16, 1932 Dian Fossey is born in San Francisco, California.

1938 Dian's parents divorce.

1939 Mother Kitty marries wealthy businessman Richard Price.

1949 Graduates from high school; enters Marin Junior College; studies business; although mother and stepfather are wealthy, they don't support her financially.

1950 Takes job at a dude ranch in Montana; has to leave job because of illness, but realizes that she wants to work with animals for a living; enrolls in a pre-veterinary program at University of California, Davis.

1952 Begins studies in occupational therapy at San Jose State College.

1954 Graduates with degree in occupational therapy.

1955 Begins working at Kosair Crippled Children's Hospital in Louisville, Kentucky, which is 2,300 miles (3,700 kilometers) away from her mother and stepfather.

1960 Interest in Africa is fueled when close friend Mary Henry returns from a trip to Rhodesia (now Zimbabwe) and shares experience.

1963 Takes first trip to Africa; meets with John Alexander, British hunter she has hired as her personal guide through Africa; meets famed archaeologist and paleontologist Louis Leakey, who arranges for her to tour archaeological sites; sets out to climb Mount Mikeno, in the Virunga Mountains in Congo with two armed rangers and 11 porters carrying gear.

1966 Meets Louis Leakey for second time, when he comes to Louisville; he asks her to undertake a long-term study of mountain gorillas; quits her job at Kosair; has her appendix removed; returns to Africa to study mountain gorillas; spends Christmas with Jane Goodall.

1967 Sets up her first research camp, Kabara, in the Virunga Mountains of Congo; sees her first group of gorillas within days of arriving; encounters poachers for first time; is forced to leave Kabara because of political unrest in the area; establishes her second research camp, called Karisoke, on the Rwanda side of the Virunga Mountains; her sometimes-boyfriend, Alexie Forrester, arrives to take her back to the United States; Dian refuses to go with him.

1968 Dian's birth father, George, kills himself; *National Geographic* magazine sends photographer Bob Campbell to document Dian's work at Karisoke.

1969 Takes in two orphaned baby gorillas, Coco and Pucker; is forced to give up Coco and Pucker; they are transferred to a zoo in Germany.

1970 Becomes first human to "hold hands" with a gorilla; Bob Campbell photographs the moment; *National Geographic* runs the first article and set of photos about Dian and her work with mountain gorillas; leaves Karisoke to begin work on her Ph.D. in Cambridge, England.

1972 Bob Campbell leaves Karisoke for last time; Louis Leakey dies from a heart attack.

1974 or 1976 Earns her Ph.D. in zoology from Cambridge University.

1977 Poachers kill Dian's favorite gorilla, Digit.

1978 Digit's death is top story on CBS evening news; Dian creates the Digit Fund; Uncle Bert and Macho are killed; their baby, Kweli, is wounded in the attack; he dies three months later.

1980 Dian moves to Ithaca, New York, to take a job at Cornell University; makes a quick visit to Karisoke; discovers her pet monkey Kima has died; returns to Ithaca with her elderly dog Cindy.

1981 Finishes writing *Gorillas in the Mist*.

1983 Returns to Karisoke; as happy as she is to reunite with members of her staff, is upset to find the camp in state of disrepair; *Gorillas in the Mist* is published; embarks on a six-month promotional tour to the United States, the UK, and South Africa.

1984 Returns to Karisoke, where she intends to spend the rest of her life; Humane Society of the United States gives Dian an award for her work with gorillas.

1985
March: Humane Society of New York gives Dian special gold medal in honor of her conservation work.

Summer: Makes her last trip to the United States; goes to California to speak at a fundraising dinner, appear on *The Tonight Show*, visit her parents, and have eye surgery.

September: Visits gorillas for the last time.

December 27: Dian is found brutally murdered in her cabin.

December 31: Dian Fossey is buried next to Digit in a graveyard beside her cabin at Karisoke.

Glossary

anthropology The study of the origins and development of humankind, especially its societies and cultures

appendicitis An inflammation of the appendix

appendix A small sac attached to the large intestine

apprehensive Anxious or nervous that something bad will happen

barrage An overwhelming quantity of something that comes at you quickly

barricade A barrier that prevents people or vehicles from passing

bloodthirsty Eager to take part in violence or killing

clamor To insist or request, urgently and forcefully

deforestation Cutting down trees or forests

dehydrated Lacking water in the body

downfall A drop in status, reputation, or power

elusive Hard to find

erratic Unpredictable, irregular

extradition Surrendering a person from one country to another, usually in order to face trial or punishment for a crime

fauna The animals of a particular region

flora The plants of a particular region

genocide The deliberate killing of a group of people, usually people of a particular race or religion

groundbreaking Innovative, pioneering

habitat The natural environment of a plant or animal

habituate To become accustomed to something by regular, long-term exposure

hyrax A small, chubby mammal about the size of a groundhog but related to the elephant

immunity The ability of an animal to resist, or fight off, an illness or disease

immunization Providing a substance, usually a vaccine, to a person for protection from a certain illness or disease

impala A small African antelope that can run quickly and leap great distances

intervene To step into a difficult situation to help change the course of the situation; to come between opposing groups to help settle their differences

intrepid Fearless, adventurous

malign To speak badly about something or someone; to criticize

mimic To imitate

musk A strong-smelling substance formed in the glands of certain animals

palette A range of colors

pre-veterinary program A set of educational courses a person must pass to be accepted into veterinary college

preconception An idea or opinion based on inadequate information or experience

prestigious Considered important, impressive, and worthy of respect

rent Past tense of *rend*: to violently tear apart, rip, or shatter; to disturb the air with loud noise

republic A state or country that is governed by a person or group elected by its citizens; a country not ruled by a king or queen

respiratory Related to breathing

rustic Simple, rough, related to the countryside

Serengeti Plains A massive region in north Tanzania and southwestern Kenya; the site of the world's largest annual mammal migration.

simultaneously Happening at the same time

Sir Galahad The purest, most noble knight in King Arthur's court

stress fracture A tiny crack in a bone, caused by repeated activity rather than sudden force

swagger To walk or conduct oneself in a confident, cocky, self-important manner

symposium A public meeting or conference organized to discuss a particular subject

talisman An object believed to bring good luck to its owner, or to ward off evil

tattoo A rapid, repeated, rhythmic drumming or tapping

telegram A form of communication that existed before telephones; a message sent by telegraph, then printed out and delivered by hand

tick A small, blood-sucking insect that can attach itself to an animal's skin; often carries disease

ungainly Awkward, clumsy

viral Caused by a virus, a microorganism that invades living cells and multiplies

vocalization A sound made for the purpose of communicating

voice actor A performer who provides the voice of an animated character

wildebeest A large, stocky, horned member of the antelope family

zoologist A scientist who studies animals

Further Information

Books

de la Bédoyère, Camilla. *No One Loved Gorillas More: Dian Fossey: Letters from the Mist*. Vancouver: Raincoast Books, 2005.

Doak, Robin S. *Dian Fossey: Friend to Africa's Gorillas* (Women in Conservation). Chicago: Heinemann Library, 2015.

Fossey, Dian. *Gorillas in the Mist*. Boston: Houghton Mifflin, 1983.

Kushner, Jill Menkes. *Who on Earth Is Dian Fossey?: Defender of the Mountain Gorillas* (Scientists Saving the Earth). Berkeley Heights, NJ: Enslow Publishers, 2010.

Mowat, Farley. *Woman in the Mists: The Story of Dian Fossey and the Mountain Gorillas of Africa*. New York: Warner Books, 1987. (Published in Canada as *Virunga: The Passion of Dian Fossey*. Toronto: McLelland & Stewart, 1987).

Nicholson, Lois. *Dian Fossey: Primatologist* (Women in Science). New York: Chelsea House, 2003.

Redmond, Ian. *Gorilla, Monkey & Ape*. New York: Dorling Kindersley, 2000.

Video/DVDs

Mountain Gorillas' Survival: Dian Fossey's Legacy Lives On (online video). Craghoppers and the Dian Fossey Gorilla Fund International, 2014. This 15-minute video is an excellent film about Dian, her work, and her legacy. Here is a link:
http://video.nationalgeographic.com/video/short-film-showcase/mountain-gorillas-survival-dian-fosseys-legacy-lives-on

Gorillas in the Mist (DVD). Universal Pictures, 1988/1999. This Hollywood film version of Dian Fossey's book, with Sigourney Weaver playing Dian, was well received by critics and audiences, although many people believe it oversimplified Dian's character.

Mountain Gorilla. (DVD/Blu-ray and online video). BBC Earth, 2010. You can buy copies of this video, but you need to be sure it is compatible with your DVD player. Here is a link to 27 different clips from the full-length documentary: **http://www.bbc.co.uk/programmes/b00rbvz2**

Websites

http://gorillafund.org/
This is the official website of the Dian Fossey Gorilla Fund International. Here, you will find the history of Karisoke, with information about the research station today. You will find blog posts, news, and information about the organization's programs, and ways you can help mountain gorillas today.

http://wwf.panda.org/what_we_do/endangered_species/ great_apes/gorillas/mountain_gorilla/ http://www.worldwildlife.org/species/mountain-gorilla
These two World Wildlife Fund sites (one international, one American) feature quick facts about mountain gorillas, along with links to other, related articles.

http://animals.nationalgeographic.com/animals/mammals/ mountain-gorilla/
Like the WWF sites, this National Geographic site is another good place to start if you're interested in mountain gorillas. It has an excellent series of photos and even a short sound clip of a mountain gorilla yelling!

Index

About the Author

Diane Dakers was born and raised in Toronto, and now makes her home in Victoria, British Columbia. Diane has been a newspaper, magazine, television, and radio journalist since 1991. She has written two fiction and 15 non-fiction books for young people.